From Bean Street to Cruise Line Captain
and Beyond

From Bean Street to Cruise Line Captain and Beyond

by

Charles Anderson

DIADEM BOOKS

From Bean Street to Cruise Line Captain and Beyond

Published by Diadem Books
Distribution coordination by Spiderwize

For information, please contact:

Diadem Books
Mews Cottage
The Causeway
KENNOWAY
Kingdom of Fife
KY8 5JU
Scotland UK

www.diadembooks.com

ISBN: 978-0-9559852-4-9

Epigraph

If I flew away beyond the east or lived in the farthest place in the west, you would be there to lead me…

Psalm 139: 9-10 (GNB)

Table of Contents

Acknowledgements ix

Preface xi

Chapter One: From Birth to Evacuation.................................... 1

Chapter Two: Schooldays 15

Chapter Three: Apprenticeship Years 23

Chapter Four: Deck Officer Years 33

Chapter Five: Cargo Ship Captain Years 43

Chapter Six: Passenger Ship Captain Years - *S.S. Veracruz* 95

Chapter Seven: Passenger Ship Captain Years - *S.S. Liberte* 125

Chapter Eight: Life After Polynesia 148

Chapter Nine: Born Again 163

Appendix 179

Acknowledgements

First of all, I want to thank my wife Jacquie for keeping a Spiritual Diary so that I have been able to quote exact dates when referring to incidents in our Christian life. She is so organized and has given me a "gee up" when I haven't felt like going on with the writing.

My daughter Susan and son-in-law Carl Saxby have been a great help in coming to my rescue when I have got out of depth with my computer, losing whole chapters which seem to have been recovered by them as if by magic. In fact, I couldn't have completed this book without their help. They have spent innumerable hours fiddling around with the photographs and items for the Appendix so that the older photos are clearer, and organising them in a semblance of order. I have learnt to follow their strict instructions: "Just type and save, don't do anything else!" From the foregoing you will probably realise that I am not "computer literate". My granddaughter Kaylee has given me some lessons on the computer and reiterates the instructions, "Just type and save!" She's very bossy but a lovely, caring young lady.

I also wish to thank my friends Captain Dennis Thompson, B.Sc (Hons)., D.M.S., Extra Master for allowing me to use information from his book, *A History of Hull Trinity House School* and Professor Donald Woodward, honorary archivist of Hull Trinity House, for giving me permission to use information from his booklet, *The Trinity House of Kingston upon Hull*.

My thanks for allowing me to reproduce photographs contained in the book are extended to the Hull Trinity House School and the Hull Trinity House Board of Trustees.

Thanks are in order to the Hull *Daily Mail*, who hold the copyright of the photograph showing Bean Street in about the year 1932, for allowing me to reproduce the photograph as the main background of the cover. Thanks are also in order to Messrs Innes, of Hessle, who have kindly allowed me to reproduce a copyright photograph on the back cover of the book which shows me in my Hull Trinity House Master Warden's regalia.

Finally, I wish to thank my friend Charles H. Muller, PhD, D.Litt, DEd., CEO of Diadem Books, who has edited this book. It is some years ago that Charles suggested I should write some of my Christian experiences down, so I've gone the whole hog and written this autobiography. Better late than never!

Preface

Everyone has an interesting story of his or her life to tell but not many people record it on paper. I remember my father, who was a boatswain or Petty Officer in the Merchant Navy, telling me stories of when he was a beachcomber in Australia with his friend Harry, a fellow Norwegian. Harry later immigrated to America and ended up being an Official of the Seafarers Union. Dad continued a seagoing career, making a few dollars in America as a boxer during the Second World War, while he was waiting for the completion of a ship being built and many other interesting interludes during his time as a seafarer. He started his sea career in sailing ships and graduated from ordinary seaman to able seaman, sail maker and then boatswain (pronounced Bosun). When I was about 12-years-old and my father came home on leave, he would instruct me in sewing canvas and the different stitches, fancy knots in rope which was an intricate part of seamanship in sailing ship times. These lessons stood me in good stead when I started my sea career, especially when I became Captain on passenger vessels because I made fancy canvas sides and knots to the passengers' gangway and an intricate covering of the steel handrails with a very effective design of canvas strips called cross pointing or coach whipping, covered with fancy knots. It had a practical purpose to prevent hands slipping on wet rails. I always had a large audience of passengers wanting to learn the skills; it was an extra activity for them.

At the beginning of the Second World War my mother volunteered for the Civil Defence, driving an ambulance and she had interesting stories of driving the ambulances during air-raid blitzes on Hull, which were rather hair-raising.

My brother Ernie first went to sea as a Galley Boy, then Deck Boy until he gained a rating as Able Seaman. He then took a correspondence course from Southampton Collage of the Sea to learn the intricacies of navigation, took the examinations for his various Mates Certificate and finally his Master's Certificate. That is the hard way to achieve progress in a sea career.

I am sorry that mum, dad and my brother did not record their experiences to pass on because those experiences, as stories, are lost forever. My brother Ernie could have written a "best seller" because he had a more interesting life than I, but he died in April 2009 and I am the only remaining original Anderson left. That's why I am recording some of my life experiences, so that my children, grandchildren and their grandchildren will have a record of my life. Everyone should do it!

I am dedicating this book to my mum, dad, family and also to the Hull Trinity House Navigation School, who gave me a thorough grounding in nautical subjects, without which I would not have had a successful sea career. The book covers the period from my birth to the present time because I have-not "popped my clogs" yet.

I am entitling the book *FROM BEAN STREET TO CRUISE LINE CAPTAIN AND BEYOND*. Bean Street was a Street in Kingston Upon Hull, Yorkshire, England, off Hessle and Anlaby Roads, which was in the heart of the fishing Industry and I was a Cruise Line Captain when I retired from a sea career. The Beyond part are my activities after I retired.

Chapter One

From Birth to Evacuation

I **WAS BORN** without complications, at the Hedon Road Maternity Hospital in Kingston upon Hull, on the 26th of November 1932, a bouncing baby boy of 8 lbs something. My father, Carl Johan Andersen, was a Norwegian Seaman and became a naturalised British subject in February 1936, when his surname Andersen became Anderson. My mother Doris, whose maiden name was Harris, was English and born in Kingston-upon-Hull. I also had a sibling Brother named Ernest Alan who was five years older than me.

Mum in her Civil Defence uniform of the ambulance service.

Mum, Dad, brother Ernie and me.

We lived in a rented house at 158, Bean Street, which was originally called New Jarratt Street but renamed Bean Street after Alderman Robert Bean who was chairman of the Corporation Property Committee.

Bean Street ran between Hessle Road and Anlaby Road, a distance of about half a mile, with terraces radiating from the main street. There must have been about two thousand people living in that area, and it seemed as if most of them were children. There was Sir Henry Cooper School, various shops, public houses, a Church opposite the School (which was bombed in the Second World War) and a pawnbroker with several secondhand shops.

Children of Tichbourne Terrace, Bean Street, c1937. Cousin Ken Harris second from the left, me in the middle between the girls.

Most of the male adults were seafarers, either in the Royal Navy, Merchant Navy, Trawler men or employed on the fish docks, unloading or servicing the fishing trawlers. Some of the female adults made extra cash by making fishing nets. It was a close-knit community, quite unique really; doors were not locked, with neighbours in and out of each other's house, playing cards, gossiping, baby-sitting. The Public Houses were the centre of social life. Family relatives lived near each other and "grandma" or "granddad" usually lived with one of their grown-up children.

Two families who were close neighbours were the Hardys and O'Donnalds. We were especially friendly with the Hardys. Mrs Hardy had two daughters, as I remember, Jean and Sheila. Jean, I believe, had suffered with polio and as a result had one leg in callipers. I was a bit sweet on Jean even at six years old and used to put my arm around her shoulders as we walked and say, "Can you manage?" That became a popular saying between the families.

There was not much road traffic in those days and the street was a playground for the children. The nearest green field areas were Pickering Park and West Park about one mile away, so the street was used as a play area more often than the parks

A greengrocer came around a couple of times a week touting his wares from a horse and cart and on a Sunday morning a baker came around selling hot cakes.

Momentous national occasions such as the 1935 Silver Jubilee were celebrated by the people with a party—not just one party, but it seemed that every terrace down Bean Street held parties. In fact, any excuse resulted in a street party.

1935 Silver Jubilee party, Tichbourne Terrace, Bean Street; me
second from left front row.

When election time for City Councillors came round, there would be a parade up and down the street, composed mainly of children, singing and encouraging everyone to vote for their favourite man. I still remember the song but not the name of the candidate. It went like this:

> Vote, vote, vote for Mr. Tadpole (or whoever it was)
> You can't vote for a better man,
> Mr. Tadpole is the man,
> And we'll have him if we can,
> And we'll throw all the others in the Dock, Dock, Dock.

It was quite an exciting occasion for the kids, the parade being led by an adult flag carrier; it seemed to go on for ages.

My mum told me the story of the time when I was just a baby. My brother Ernie had just got a bicycle for his birthday and he was told to look after me. Some time later a neighbour came to tell her Ernie was riding up and down the street with the pram tied on the back of his bike. Ernie had his bike confiscated for about a week.

Another time, when I was about 5-years-old, I remember this occasion very clearly; my brother Ernie and his pals were going to Pickering Park and my mum told Ernie that he had to take me as well or he couldn't go. Ernie met his pals who said, "What's he coming for?" Ernie explained he had to bring me but the gang made me walk behind them as if I wasn't with them. On the way to the park, we came to a sweet shop and the gang made me go into the shop and steal some sweets. Fortunately, I wasn't caught but I can still remember stealing those sweets.

As a youngster, I always seemed to have a runny nose and throat problems, as all the kids did in those days. I went into hospital to have my tonsils and adenoids removed which seemed to be the corrective measure at that time. In hospital, it was like a production line and after the operation I woke up in a ward full of kids who had been "done". One would start crying, which triggered the others to start crying. How the nurses could stand being on that ward I will never know—they deserved a big medal! Even when they brought ice cream round to sooth our throats, it didn't make the slightest difference to the level of crying.

My brother Ernie was my role model and I followed him wherever he went. I must have been a nuisance. Once, I followed him to school and the teachers had to send for my mum. I remember crying all the way home, saying I wanted to go to school.

At this time it was common practice that when any of the family died, usually their body was laid out in an open casket in the front room and curtains drawn shut. Family and friends would come to the house to pay their last respects and the cortege and mourners would leave from the house for the burial. The front room was only used for special occasions, such as parties, bodies laid out and wakes.

I remember when my grandmother died, she was laid out in our front room and I went to see her. Grandma was the first dead body I had seen but it wasn't to be the last. She was dressed in her best clothes, her face grey, wax like and when I kissed her she was very cold.

Just before war was declared in 1939, it was considered lucky if you could touch the collar on the back of a sailor's uniform. We had plenty of opportunities because there were plenty of Royal Navy sailors down Bean Street.

War was declared on the 3rd of September 1939, when I was 6-years-old. Hull being a large port was considered a prime target for the Germans to bomb, and arrangements were made to evacuate all the children out of Hull to country locations with less risk of being bombed. I remember being mustered at the school and joining a queue to board a bus complete with gas mask and luggage label tied to my coat collar with my name and other information written on it for identification. The mums were all crying, and the children were excited and also crying—what a racket! Some mums and teachers boarded the bus as escorts.

Off we went on our adventure, heading towards Hinderwell in North Yorkshire. We made a stop for lunch in Whitby on our way and arrived at Hinderwell in the afternoon. We were all mustered in the Chapel Hall at Hinderwell, where a group of villagers were waiting. It was all quite orderly and the person in charge had a list in his hand and commenced to call out names. The named person came forward and chose the number of evacuees they had stated they could take, usually one, sometimes two. I was quite a big lad for my age, so I stood as tall as I could, thinking that I would stand out in the crowd and have a better chance of being chosen. It took me some time to realise the people were choosing mainly girls and not many boys; also, they were choosing the smaller ones! After about three quarters of the evacuees had been chosen and only boys left, I thought I was going to be left, so I tried to make myself look smaller by bending my knees, but it didn't work. Then there were only two boys left—me and a boy called David. Everyone except the person in charge had gone and we were left on our own. Then a lady called Mrs Jackson arrived and made her apologies to the person in charge for being late. She told him she really had wanted to take two girls as all her grown up children were male, but she took us and off we went to a coastal village called Port Mulgrave, about two miles from Hinderwell. The house was at the beginning of a long row of houses; actually, the address was 8 Long Row, Port Mulgrave. The village was situated at the top of a high steep cliff, the cliff meeting the stony beach with a small harbour adjacent about 500 feet below.

Mr and Mrs Jackson were Christians and they took us into their home and treated us like one of their own, with love and affection. We attended Chapel on a Sunday as a family and I couldn't have been billeted with anyone more considerate and caring.

Mr & Mrs Jackson with me and their young grandson.

Three things stick out in my mind—well, four really! On one occasion, a school day, I must have eaten something that had disagreed with me. At the break time I wanted to go to the toilets but they were all occupied and I had an accident and messed my trousers. I cleaned myself up the best I could but the smell was horrible! When the break time was over, we went back to the classroom and within a minute the teacher, crinkling her nose, inquired, "Who has made that smell?" It was pretty obvious really because there was a ring of empty chairs around me. I owned up and the teacher told me to go home. It was a two-mile walk and I had to hold the bottom of my short trousers tightly because my upset stomach was still misbehaving and I cried all the way home. When I arrived at Mrs Jackson's, she stood me in a tin bath and cleaned me up. I was so grateful she hadn't been annoyed and she was quite understanding and comforting.

The second occasion was when my Mum and Dad arrived at Port Mulgrave to take me away on holiday for a while. My Dad had docked in Middlesbrough after being away for 18 months and the ship was in dry-dock so my parents thought it was a good opportunity to take me on holiday. I hadn't seen my Mum for about 9 months and my Dad for 18 months and I had just come home from school and there was my Mum and Dad waiting for me. I said, "What have you come for?" I can still see the shock on their faces at these first words. Kids can be cruel with words. I suppose I was just landing out at them vocally for being away so long.

The third occasion was when a sea mine had been washed up on the beach. I and a couple of my friends went down the beach, took shelter behind a rock and threw stones at the sea mine. Fortunately, the mine didn't blow up and a home guard person chased us off.

The fourth occasion is the kindness of Mr and Mrs Jackson during the time I was in their care. I was just like a son to them.

I stayed with the Jacksons for about two years until the German air-raids got too frequent and we were regularly disturbed at night to take shelter under the stairs of the house. Because of this, my mum thought it was best if I was relocated to Eastrington where my brother and the older children of Sir Henry Cooper School had been evacuated; and it would also be possible to visit me more frequently there because Eastrington was in the country and only about twenty miles from Hull.

Sir Henry Cooper school evacuees, Eastrington. Me far left second row & brother Ernie fifth from left back row.

I went to Eastrington and was billeted with a Family called Grebby. The house with a smallholding and numerous outbuildings was quite large, about five bedrooms, with an attic, cellar, front room, dining room, kitchen and an outhouse toilet with no running water. During the winter you had to be desperate to visit the toilet because the trip from the house to the toilet was so cold and you didn't hang around reading the newspaper very long. Cooking and water heating was done on the dining room fire. A well with a manual pump in the kitchen provided fresh water and a 200-gallon steel drum was situated outside the kitchen to collect rainwater for washing clothes.

There was no heating except for the dining room fire and in the winter, it was so cold, frost patterns formed inside the house on the windowpanes. Having no electricity, lighting was provided by paraffin lamps and candles. A radio powered by a wet battery provided news and entertainment and every week the battery was charged up at the local garage.

My brother Ernie and Cousin Ken Harris were also billeted at Mrs Grebby's with three other evacuees, so I made the sixth. Four of us slept in the same bedroom in two large beds, two occupying a bed. The other two occupied a bed in the attic. During the winter when the weather was exceptionally cold, we had hot bricks wrapped in towels put in our beds about half an hour before we went to bed to warm the bed clothing up. We had a bath once a week, sharing the same bath water, because it was a major operation getting the hot water transferred from the dining room into the kitchen. The hot water was heated in the dining room fireplace, ladled out of the water-heating receptacle into a bucket and carried into the kitchen, and then poured into a tin bath. The youngest bathed first; then we bathed in order of age. The water was a bit soapy, cloudy and almost cold for the last bather.

Mr Grebby was retired and Mrs Grebby was crippled with arthritis, but still active, doing all the cooking, washing and cleaning with the help of her two daughters but never complaining about the pain she must have been enduring. She was the boss of the house without question. The two adult daughters, Joan aged about 22, who had a baby boy, Robert, and Annie aged about 30, helped in the house. Joan was married to a soldier called Robert Jackson who was on active service and Annie, besides helping in the house, had a job working on a farm. Unfortunately, Annie had a cleft pallet and her speech was distorted and hard to understand, but she had a heart of gold.

Life was never dull in the village and the accent was on helping the war effort, "digging for victory" it was called. Everyone planted vegetables instead of flowers and if they had sufficient land or outbuildings, chickens and pigs were reared. Mrs Grebby had chickens and reared pigs in the outbuildings, which we helped to feed, but a strict official control was exercised as to the disposal of the pigs when they had grown big enough to slaughter; in fact, when Mrs Grebby had one of her pigs killed for her own use, she had to surrender six months' bacon coupons on the ration card for all of us.

It seemed as if everything going on in the village was geared to the war effort. Mrs Grebby gave me permission to cultivate a patch of land in the orchard to grow vegetables on. I grew lettuce, cabbages, sprouts and potatoes. When they were ready for harvesting, some went into the provision of the house, some I sold and I would take a bagful to my mum whenever I went home which was about once a month for the weekend when I was older. I also used to gather mushrooms, some as large as dinner plates, just before I went home, so I was pretty loaded with vegetables and mushrooms when I boarded the bus or sometimes the train to Hull.

I had a bad experience coming back to Eastrington by train one Sunday night. We arrived in Eastrington station and the carriage door was jammed and wouldn't open. Before one of the adults in the carriage could attract the train guard's attention the train moved off. The next stop was at a village called Howden, about five miles from Eastrington. The guard's attention couldn't be attracted so one of the adults dropped down the carriage window and pushed me out onto the platform. I had a long walk back to Eastrington and by the time I arrived at Mrs. Grebby's it was about 11 p.m. and everyone was in bed, asleep. I had to make a bit of a racket to wake someone up and let me in. I didn't have a very great reception and just went straight to bed.

I was quite interested in farm animals and would spend some time at one farm, "mucking out" the pigs and being a general "dogsbody". The farmer gave me a few pence every week for my help and at Christmas gave me a chicken that was dead but wasn't plucked, to take home to my mum.

I also earned one shilling (5 new pence) every Saturday for working two hours at the local general stores shop, weighing two pounds of sugar out from large sacks into blue paper sugar bags.

At this time everyone was encouraged to buy National Savings Certificates to help the war effort. With the money I earned and saved from weighing out sugar, potato picking, pea picking, selling my vegetables and "mucking out", I managed to buy four Certificates which cost fifteen shillings each (that's 75p in new currency). After ten years they were worth one pound and six pence each. (That's one pound 2½p in new currency.) I still have one of them. I don't know if I would be paid compound interest if I was to cash it in but it's better as a memento of my war effort when I was evacuated.

The school had a large allotment where the schoolchildren spent quite a good deal of their time, digging, planting, sowing and reaping throughout the year. In autumn the schoolchildren went out, en masse, collecting rosehips which were sold and money donated to the war effort.

I remember one day two large barrels of red apples were delivered at the school, which had been sent from the people of Canada. The children got two apples each. All the kids were excited; it wasn't because of the apples—we already had orchards full of apples—but because they had come from Canada! It provided a focal point for the teachers to give us a Geography and Letter Writing lesson because we all wrote a letter of thanks.

Money raising programmes were organised to collect enough money to buy a Fighter Aeroplane called the Spitfire. I think the cost of the Spitfire was subscribed to by several villages, which promoted a competitive spirit. One of the several events organised by Eastrington was an auction on the village green, where people donated items which the villagers would bid for. I was only about 9-years-old but I remember bidding 6 old pence for a live rabbit. I think the villagers wanted me to have it and didn't out-bid me, so I bought myself a live rabbit which I had for about a year until it escaped from its hutch. It was a doe and must have mated with a wild buck rabbit because there appeared crossbred young rabbits in the orchard at a later date.

There was an Italian prisoner of war camp quite near and the inmates volunteered as farm labourers to earn a little cash. Some of the prisoners worked on the farm where Annie worked. One of them took a shine to Annie who was confused and elated because she'd never had a boyfriend before. I think Annie wanted to bring the man to meet Mrs Grebby and the family but Mrs Grebby was really annoyed and forbade her to see the man again. I remember Annie crying as if her heart were broken and pleading with Mrs Grebby to let her keep seeing the Italian, but all to no avail.

During the war, if anyone was killed on active service, the war department sent a telegram informing the next of kin and everyone knew what the delivery by the postman of a telegram meant. Joan's husband, Robert, was due on leave when the postman delivered a telegram to Joan. She brought it into the kitchen, opened it, and then fainted. Mrs Grebby took charge, read the telegram and brought Joan back to consciousness. "Pull yourself together," Mrs Grebby instructed Joan, "The telegram only says that Robert is going to be delayed one day." Joan had fainted before she read the telegram because she thought it was going to tell her Robert had been killed in action!

I was quite a good singer and in the church choir. Choir practice was every Thursday evening and lasted about one hour, practising psalms and hymns. A musical festival was held annually at North Cave, a village about ten miles from Eastrington. The choirmaster persuaded me to enter the Boys' Solo age 10 to 11 category. This was in 1944. There were quite a number of boys entered for the competition and I was the third singer. I remember the occasion vividly! The song was, "I saw three ships come sailing by." Half way through the song my voice broke and I stopped singing. With encouragement from the Adjudicator, I started singing again and managed to croak my way to the end. When I came off the stage, a lady put her arm around me and said, "Never mind dear, you did your best!" The remaining boys waiting to sing seemed to take fright and wouldn't even go on the stage, so only three of us sang in our category. The first boy got 95 Marks, the second 93 marks and I came third out of three with 80 marks—it must have been for effort! I still have the certificate to prove it!

Most of the able bodied men had been called up for active service and the farmers hired local women, Land Army girls, Italian prisoners of war and older schoolchildren for the planting and harvesting of crops. The main crops were potatoes, peas, sugar beet and wheat. I was involved with planting and harvesting all these food items. I liked potato picking the best of all. A horse-drawn machine with two rotating circular steel gadgets with curved steel rods radiating from the centre dug into the earth and scattered the potatoes on the ground. The potatoes were gathered in large wickerwork baskets by a team of labourers following the machine. As the baskets were filled, they were taken to a farm labourer following the group who emptied the baskets into a horse-drawn cart.

With the baskets resting on the ground, especially in wet weather, the bottom of the baskets were caked with soil and became too heavy to carry, so the labourer in charge of the horse and cart would remove the soil with a big knife. When the cart was full, the cart was taken to a suitable location in the field and the potatoes tipped on the ground. As successive loads of potatoes were tipped, eventually a long triangular shape was formed, which was covered with straw, the straw then being covered by soil dug from the ground near the sides of the "Potato Pie", which formed a soak-away for rain water. The potatoes could then be taken from this storage system as required. At the end of the day, the carts were left in the field and horses taken to the farms for stabling, feeding and watering. The labourers in charge of the horses let us kids ride them back to the farm—two, sometimes three to a horse, because they were not little piddling horses, but big strong shire horses, built for work.

One day after work, when I had a ride on one of the horses and the farm hands were in the stables, taking off the horse's bridles and bits, they asked me if I wanted a "plough boy's eight". I didn't know what they were talking about but said yes. Two of the farm hands grabbed me and thrust me head first into the horse's bum. I was terrified and was screaming and shouting but they thought it was a good joke; the horse didn't pay any attention and just kept on eating its supper of oats as if it was used to it. I had nightmares for ages afterwards.

For one day's hard labour potato picking, the children were paid half a crown, which in today's currency is 12 and a half pence. Pea picking was paid by weight. The peas were pulled and put in big sacks. When a sack was full, it was carried to the responsible farm hand who weighed it and paid according to the weight. Some of the workers hid lumps of soil in the bag to increase the weight. I didn't, though—well, maybe once or twice. The going rate for picking a sack full of peas was sixpence, equivalent to 2 and a half pence in today's currency.

I had one or two ailments while billeted with Mrs Grebby in addition to the usual infestation of head lice.

One night I had a very bad earache and Mrs Grebby heated a large onion, covered it in a cloth and tied it to my ear. It seemed to ease the pain and I managed to get to sleep. I suppose a brick would have done just as well because it must have been the heat that treated the earache.

Another time I somehow contracted impetigo and was sent to an isolation hospital in Snaith, a village about fifteen miles from Eastrington. Impetigo is a very contagious skin disease marked by isolated pustules around the face and hands, which become crusted and ruptured. On arrival at the hospital, a bath was made ready and I was placed in the bath and the pustules were scrubbed with a large nailbrush until they bled. It was readily painful. When all the pustules had been made to bleed, I was made to get out of the bath, and then the bleeding areas were painted with some concoction that stung and was more painful than the scrubbing. I had this treatment on a regular basis until the pustules did not reappear. Needless to say, I dreaded the corrective treatment. I was in the isolation hospital for about two weeks before being gratefully taken back into the care of Mrs Grebby.

Eastrington was in the flight path for aircraft going and returning from bombing raids to Europe. On one occasion one of the aircraft couldn't make it back to the airfield and crash landed quite near the village. Everyone went to view the wreckage and I collected some bullets before the R.A.F. sent security guards to surround the aircraft. I later tried to detonate the bullets by hammering a nail at the base of the bullet but fortunately it didn't work. Some of the Italian prisoners of war collected shattered Perspex and fashioned rings out of the material, selling them on to the locals as souvenirs.

The village had a company of Home Guard who often had war exercises against other village Home Guard companies. Whenever this happened, it seemed as if it was a chance to experience a little bit of excitement and quite a crowd would gather to watch the war games. I remember on one occasion a lorry came through the village, approached the Eastrington Home Guard mobile headquarters and, as they passed, a shower of make-believe bombs filled with flour were thrown by the opposing forces, supposedly demolishing the headquarters.

By 1944 the German air raids on Hull had eased. My Mum had resigned from her job in the civil defence as an ambulance driver so I returned home.

My time as an evacuee living in the country away from my family was quite an experience, but it's an experience I wouldn't have missed for anything.

Chapter Two

Schooldays

DURING THE TIME I had been evacuated, Mum had moved house twice, due to being "bombed out" of the previous homes and we now lived at 32 Stirling Street, Anlaby Road, Kingston upon Hull. I was 11 and so the first objective was to find me a local school to attend. The only school with any vacancies was a school called Newington High School, which shared the buildings with a school called Eastfield Road School, about a mile and a half away from where I lived. I caught a bus or more likely walked to and from school. At first, I stayed for school dinners, for which we were charged sixpence but the dinners were so bad I spent my sixpence on fresh baked bread cakes from a local shop. It must have been a gold mine because nearly all the school kids did the same, except for the kids who were entitled to free school meals, such as sons and daughters of dads and mums in the forces, or children from very poor families.

In those days, you went to a school at 5 years of age and stayed at the same school until you had completed your education at 14 or had passed examinations, called 11 plus examinations to attend schools for higher education.

I well remember my first day at Newington. We had an outdoor games period of "touch" rugby, where the holder of the rugby ball couldn't be tackled but had to give the ball over when touched. I was quite a big lad for my age and good at sports. One of the boys known as "Fatty Rawson" (I know it isn't socially correct to emphasize physical disabilities/abnormalities but that is what kids did in those days, and probably still do. Kids can be cruel), had the ball and no one was trying to tag him so I tagged him. His face was like thunder! "I'll see you after school in the field," he snarled. I didn't know what he meant so asked one of the other boys. "Oh, I wouldn't like to be in your shoes, he's going to beat you up!" he explained. News of the incident went around the school like wildfire and at 3.45 p.m. the field was crowded with the whole school. The "cock" of the school, that's the top fighter, who was 14 years old was present to officiate and started off the fight. I landed a couple of punches and Rawson started running away with me in pursuit. The "cock" of the school stopped me and suddenly gave me a punch to my left ear, which felt like a sledgehammer and stopped me in my tracks. I suppose he was just showing me who was boss and not to try anything with him. I think that punch gave me a perforated eardrum because I've had trouble with it ever since. The next day I was called to the Headmaster's room and asked about the trouble. I explained what had happened and he told me he would be watching my future conduct, then asked me with a knowing smile who had won.

While at Newington I was picked for the school football team, which was one of the better teams in the schools league and also picked to represent Hull Schools playing against other City/Town Schools. A good school friend, Jack Ashbridge, was also chosen. I played left wing and Jack was centre half.

I had always wanted to work at sea and when I was 13, my mum and dad thought they would give me the best start possible in a sea career by applying for me to attend Hull Trinity House Navigation School.

Entrance to the school was by examination in maths, English, reading and dictation. There was a minimum height of 4 feet 6 inches. The Headmaster interviewed the parents of the prospective pupil and the pupil. If all these examinations were successful, the applicant finally had to have an eyesight and medical test before being accepted as a pupil.

From Newington there were three boys that applied to join Trinity—myself, Jack Ashbridge and Harry Sennet. We all passed the required entrance tests. Harry was quite small, just under the minimum height. We told him to stand as straight as he could and we would give him the nod if he was under, then he should go on tiptoe. Fortunately, Harry seemed to grow a couple of inches when it came for him to be measured and he made the mark—just. I don't know if he had special shoes made for the occasion.

I passed the examinations in 34th position, the penultimate position, in fact, just making it into the school by the skin of my teeth. I think my father being a seaman and my sporting achievements made the difference with the Headmaster whether I was admitted or rejected.

After being admitted to the school, there followed a three-month probationary period, after which we were issued with a uniform consisting of a pair of boots, socks, white trousers, blue trousers, shirt, waistcoat, jacket, hat and oilskin raincoat.

Trinity House pupils and teachers, 1946. Probationers at the front not in uniform, me far left.

The school had come into being in 1786, due to a shortage of qualified men and officers to crew whaling and merchant ships departing from Hull. In 1785, a committee of Trinity House Brethren was set up to examine the possibility of establishing a Marine School in the town under the jurisdiction of the Trinity House Brethren. The Hull Trinity House Navigation School was founded on the 2nd February 1786, to teach boys the art of navigation. Members of the Board of Trinity House, of whom there are 18 Brethren, sponsored two pupils each, making 36 pupils. As time went on the number of pupils increased and when I attended from 1946 to 1949, there were approximately 130. A book written by Captain Dennis Thompson, B.Sc. (Hons), Ex.C.,D.M.S. entitled, *A History of Hull Trinity House School*, gives a comprehensive account of the history of the school. He also wrote a booklet called *The Hull Trinity House School*. Captain Thompson was headmaster of the school from 1972 to 1989 inclusive. He is also an Elder Brother of the guild of Hull Trinity House.

From being a "fag" (new boy) to leaving to take up an apprenticeship with a shipping company, my time at Trinity House Navigation School was memorable. Every morning the boys were paraded in the schoolyard and inspected by the teachers as to appearance, clean boots, any missing buttons, and white collar on the jacket blankoed. The Trinity Flag was hoisted on the flagpole and saluted. Then the boys were dismissed to go to their respective classrooms. There are inspections to this day but not as thorough.

Every Sunday the boys had to attend the Holy Trinity Church and paraded in uniform from the school to the church which was quite nearby. The boys were seated down one side of the church. In the front row in the centre of the church where the rows were perpendicular to the boys, sat the girlfriends of some of the boys. The girls looking to see where their boyfriends were seated smiled and giggled away. Some of the boys had brought Sunday papers with them and during the sermon got their heads down reading the papers.

The school has a chapel and once a month, the first Wednesday in the month, the school chaplain takes a service, which is attended by the Brethren, Boys and Pensioners who reside at the Hull Trinity House Rest Homes, a charity run by the Trinity House Trustees for ex-seafarers and their dependants.

At the entrance to the Schoolyard, there was a large brick air-raid shelter, into which the older boys often crammed the "fags", and then threw stink bombs amongst them. The air-raid shelter was known as "The Black Hole of Calcutta".

Running at one side down the full length of the yard was a double barred iron rail and if a "fag" was cheeky, the older boys would twist the arms of the cheeky "fag" around the rail and apply pressure to the arms. This was known as being put on the rack.

Strict discipline was maintained by the teachers, assisted by the Captain of the School and seven Officers (known as prefects in other schools). Whenever a teacher was absent from a classroom for any reason, one of the Officers would take charge to keep order. As an Officer's vacancy occurred, the teachers, with some input from the Officers, elected a new Officer. When I left school, I had reached the rank of Second Officer.

Every month a barber would attend the school to cut all the pupils' hair. I think this concession was also open to the teachers but no one ever took up the offer. He was known as "Sweeny Todd", and must have been the worst hairdresser in the U.K., if not the world. He had a list of pupils and you had to put your signature against your name to signify that "Sweeny" had cut your hair. For each signature, he received six old pence. With about 130 heads of hair to cut he wasn't particular how the hair looked and the standard style was large steps, all over the head. The senior boys always made the excuse that they had an appointment that day at the hairdressers. So long as the boys signed their names to the paper, he didn't care. "Ted" Selby, one of the teachers, was eagle eyed and sent anyone back to "Sweeny" who didn't have a stepped haircut, much to the amusement and hilarity of the other boys in the class. After one of "Sweeny's" haircuts, most boys went to a proper barber for corrective treatment.

As you can imagine, discipline was very strict and once being admitted as a probationary Trinity Cadet, the parents were issued with a Rule Book concerning the standards of behaviour expected of the Cadet and the parents, also the consequences of not adhering to the rules.

Rule 20 concerned the dismissal of a Cadet for misconduct or for any cause whatsoever. On one occasion by the direction of the Headmaster, I had to write this rule out 10 times as a warning/punishment for smoking.

It happened like this. One Saturday afternoon I had been playing football for the school team and was on my way home, with a school friend called Ray Phillips who was our goalkeeper, who caught the same Trolley Bus, a number 69 on the Anlaby Road route. It was a bitterly cold day and I was shivering with cold. Ray said, "Here Charlie, have a ciggie, it will warm you up." He was an accomplished, experienced smoker and I had never smoked a cigarette in my life before. I took the cigarette he offered me and stuck it in my mouth. Ray lit it and I puffed away, not removing the cigarette from my mouth at all. As I said, Ray was an experienced smoker and had his cigarette cupped in his hand, bringing it to his mouth and inhaling occasionally. As we approached the number 69 trolley bus, Ray said, "Oh, there's Ted Selby on the top." I looked up and didn't have the gumption to take the cigarette out of my mouth. I could only hope that Ted hadn't seen me.

At school on Monday, I was on tenterhooks all day and when nothing had been said by 3 p.m. I thought I might have had the good fortune that Ted hadn't seen me smoking—but that was a forlorn hope. I was summoned to the Headmaster's Room and given the third degree about my smoking. I told the Headmaster it was the first time I had smoked, which was true, but he had that "I've heard it all before" look. He gave me a right rollicking about discipline and the risk of being expelled for breaking the school rules, then gave me my punishment to write out rule 20, ten times, which I had to do before I went home, with a letter for my Mum. I never smoked again while at Trinity School.

Trinity House school football team, bottom row from left: Sharpe, Robinson, Burton, Atkinson & Allison. Middle row: Barker, Lawson & Matchett. Top row: Mr. Eldon (Teacher), Ashbridge, Phillips & me.

While at Trinity I won the Captain Harris prize, which was an annual prize given for Chivalry. As part of the prize, I received a sextant in a wooden hambone case and the remainder of the prize was a book token to be redeemed at Brown's Book Store, with which I brought a book called *Boat*

Building Simplified. Unfortunately, I gave the sextant away to a Cadet on one of the ships I served as Third Officer when I bought a modern sextant, called the "Kingstonian". The Captain Harris sextant would have been worth a fortune now as an antique. The book I still have.

Me: 1949 in school uniform.

When we were approaching the end of our basic nautical education at Trinity, one of the main English Lessons was writing a letter of application to Shipping Companies for Deck Officer Apprenticeships. I wrote about 50 letters to various shipping companies asking if they had any vacancies for an Apprenticed Deck Officer. Some answered negatively, some didn't answer at all. It was my last letter of application that I learnt a lesson, which has stayed with me all my life. I wrote to a Shipping Company called W.J. Tatem of London. They answered my letter with the news that they had already contacted the Headmaster of Trinity to supply two Apprentices from the school so the vacancies had been filled. I wrote back thanking them for the information and I would be grateful if they would keep me in mind if any further vacancies occurred.

About a week later, on a Friday, I was at the school playing fields when the Headmaster sent a message for me to go back to the school immediately. When I arrived back at school the Headmaster said that he had received a telephone call from Tatems and they wanted me, as one of the two boys, to join a ship called the *Northleigh* which was dry docking in Cardiff and due to sail from Cardiff in ballast for Galveston, Texas, to load a cargo of grain on the 23rd. of February 1949.

The lesson I learnt was that whenever you are knocked back, don't just leave things as they are—do something about it and always reply to negative letters in a positive way.

The next couple of weeks were a bit hectic. Fortunately, my dad was at home on leave so was able to supervise the buying of my uniform and work clothes, signing my Apprentice's Indentures and purchasing a rail ticket to join the *S.S. Northleigh* in Cardiff. The Apprenticeship was to last four years for which I was to receive a total of £390—£75 for the first year, £90 the second year, £105 the third year and £120 the final year, with a £5 bonus (good boy bonus) paid for satisfactory service after the four-year period. I was also to receive 12 shillings per year in lieu of washing. (This refers to laundry, not personal washing!) My mum had to act as surety to the sum of £20 that I would in effect complete the four-year Apprenticeship and during that period be a "Good Boy".

On the 1st. of February 1949, I said goodbye to all my friends and teachers at Trinity House Navigation School, aged 16 years and 3 months to begin my sea career.

Chapter Three

Apprenticeship Years

A S I STATED PREVIOUSLY, the shipping company W.J.Tatems required two Apprentices, and I was one of the chosen. The other boy chosen by the Headmaster was a friend called Geoff Wood, who had taken over from Ray Phillips as goalkeeper in the football team.

We boarded the overnight train from Hull to Cardiff on the 19th February 1949, with our luggage, resplendent in Apprentice Uniforms and Greatcoats, and arrived in Cardiff about 5.30 a.m. We caught a taxi to the docks and arrived at an apparently deserted quayside except for this large cargo ship with the name *Northleigh* on its bow. It was still dark and very cold. It was low water and the gangway was leading down onto the ship's deck amidships from the quay. We both decided to step on the deck together and disturbed a couple of rats, which went scurrying off in different directions. We stood on the deck wondering what to do, when the night watchman came up to us. "Are you the new Apprentices?" he inquired. To which question we affirmed that we were. "Okay, follow me, I'll show you to your cabin," he stated.

From the deck on the port side, we entered into some enclosed accommodation through a heavy teak door. The first door we came to was a door marked APPRENTICES. "There you are," the watchman said and off he went. I opened the door, which led into a narrow room, about 3 metres by 4 metres, containing a table, two benches, and a sink, which didn't leave much floor space. A door, which was closed, led off this room. I opened the door. The room was about the same size as the first room and contained four bunks with closed bunk curtains supported by brass rods, two each side of the room, one over the other. There was a chest of drawers with four drawers directly in front of the door, four wooden lockers, two each side adjacent to the door and two benches beside the bottom bunk beds, with even less floor space than the first room. As things turned out, these two rooms were going to be my home for the next three years, because I was promoted to Third Officer for the last year of my Apprenticeship and the Third Officer's accommodation was much superior to these cramped spaces.

A top bunk light went on, the bunk curtain was pulled back and a blond haired, sleepy face appeared around the edge of the curtain. "Are you the new apprentices?" the sleepy faced person asked. "Yes Sir," I responded. "You needn't call me sir; I'm only the senior apprentice." He clambered down from the bunk onto the bench, then onto the deck. "My name is Tim," he stated. "I hope you've got working clothes besides the uniforms." We confirmed we had. "Well, pick yourselves one of the other bunks, one of the lockers and one of the drawers. The top one's mine." While Tim was getting washed in the other room and dressed in his working clothes, Geoff and I started unpacking our suitcases.

By the time we had finished unpacking our clothes and putting them into our selected locker and drawer, the time was about 7 a.m. "Come on," said Tim, "we'll go for breakfast." Geoff and I followed Tim out onto the deck. I looked up at the funnel, which had a large "T" in the centre. "I suppose that means Tatems," I remarked to Tim. "Yes," he replied, "T on the funnel and nothing on the table." It might have referred to the quality of feeding, which proved to be correct because the feeding was strictly in accordance with the minimum requirements as stated on the articles of agreement, which we signed before joining the ship. We continued into the amidships accommodation where the Captain and Deck Officers lived and the Saloon (dining area for the Officers) was situated. The Apprentices had a mess room adjacent to the Saloon. The pantry, from where the meals were served, was opposite the mess room. The Officers had waiter service but the Apprentices went to the pantry to be served.

After breakfast Tim introduced us to the Chief Officer, a small, rotund Welshman wearing a uniform cap and working clothes called Dougie Denman. "Have you got any work clothes?" he enquired—to which we confirmed (to this popular question!) that we had. "Well, you'd better get changed out of your uniform as quickly as you can because we start work at eight."

That was our introduction to the life of an Apprentice in W. J. Tatem's on board the *S.S. Northleigh*.

Three days after joining the ship, we sailed from Cardiff in ballast towards Houston, Texas, where we were to load a full cargo of wheat. The voyage started badly. We headed into a full Westerly gale, the ship rolling and pitching violently. I was on the 8 to 12 watch and received instructions from one of the A.B.'s on my watch. "Listen kid, you've got the farmer," he said. "At 11.30 go into the galley and make a pot of tea from the geyser. At one bell call the 12 to 4 watch with a cup of tea. Got it?" "Yes," I answered, but I thought, Farmer, Geyser, he's having me on! My father had told me that the crew would try to take the mickey by telling me to go somewhere for a long wait or go forward to the paint locker and ask the bosun for some green or red oil for the sidelights and thought the instructions were another mickey-taking event. However, it turned out it wasn't. Having the farmer means that you are on two-hour lookout duties, in my case from 9 p.m. to 11 p.m. The geyser was the water boiler in the cookhouse.

While on lookout, I became seasick due to the violent rolling. Unfortunately, I vomited on the weather side and my vomit splashed all over the wheelhouse doors and windows. This brought the third mate bounding up the ladder from the bridge deck to the Monkey Island. After forcefully advising me to be sick on the lee side, he could see I wasn't in any shape to take any notice of what he was saying so took pity on me and said I could go to my cabin, where I could be sick in comfort. I duly accepted this kind offer and promptly disappeared to the cabin and went to bed. At ten pasted midnight an irate seaman woke me up. "Did you call the watch?" he shouted at me. "I thought you were taking the mickey talking about the farmer and geyser," I replied meekly. He could see how I was suffering through seasickness so he just gave a resigned grunt and disappeared.

The bad weather lasted five days and so did my seasickness; then the wind became calm, the sea became smooth, I stopped being seasick and after a few days with the changed sea conditions thought, "What a great career I've chosen!"

The Captain was named Scobie, born in South Africa but married and living in Wales. He was studying for his Extra Master's Certificate, the highest nautical qualification at that time. Fortunately, he took a great interest in the training of the Apprentices and gave us study lessons every evening after tea, which also helped him with his studying. On a Sunday morning we would gather on the Monkey Island for signalling practice in Morse code and semaphore and he encouraged us to go on the bridge at night to signal any passing ships. Fortunately, Captain Scobie remained on the *Northleigh* during my four years service in Tatems.

There were many special experiences and incidents I can recall while serving on the *Northleigh*—some good, some bad and some forgettable, but all in all I enjoyed the experience of training to be a Deck Officer, and consider I was privileged to have had Captain Scobie to oversee my training.

We had several voyages, sailing from the U.K. to Vancouver, via the Panama Canal, to load grain and timber. The *Northleigh* had a top speed of 10 knots so we took about six weeks to get to Vancouver, Canada. Sailing along the Californian coast, we passed through shoal upon shoal of tuna fish. The Bosun fixed a fishing line trailing from each side the stern with a piece of red bunting as lure tied to a large hook on the end. You could see when we were approaching the shoals of tuna by the disturbance on the sea surface and we would ask the engineers to slow down as we passed through the shoals and we would catch at least three tuna each time. This happened about four times during daylight hours so we had plenty of fresh fish to eat. In fact, every day—three times a day—it was cooked in every way imaginable...broiled, boiled, fried, curried, until we became sick of the sight of fish. We asked the Chief Steward to have ordinary meat meals occasionally, which were a welcome change. Each tuna weighed about 40 lbs so there were plenty of fillets off each fish. The freezer was full of fish, which pleased the Chief Steward who was responsible for the ship's menus and feeding costs, because his feeding costs were low with us supplying our own produce.

On one of these voyages to load timber at Port Alberni on Vancouver Island, at the mouth of the river going up to Port Alberni, the salmon were running up the river and were so prolific that I'm sure you could have walked on top of the salmon without sinking in the water. It was an amazing sight. There were lots of salmon canning factories on Vancouver Island at that time in 1950, but I think most of them are derelict now.

We always had one or two of the seamen deserting the ship on these voyages, some because they had become romantically involved with local girls or they had been offered jobs. Without their passports or discharge books, which were locked up in the Captain's safe, some of them were caught and returned to England; some married Canadian girls so I think became eligible to stay in Canada. I think this story of one deserter from the *Northleigh* is intriguing.

The Second Cook, Mr Scott who had such a charming personality and was from my home town, Hull, deserted and we didn't see him for about a year, until one voyage to Vancouver he came on board to visit us and this was his story. When he deserted, he applied for a job he saw advertised in the local paper for a chimney sweep. When he attended the interview, he was asked if he knew anything about chimney sweeping. "Oh yes," he replied, "I was a chimney sweep in England," so he got the job. He became a bit fed up of being a chimney sweep and being dirty all the time, so he applied for a job as a furniture remover. "Have you any experience of furniture removing?" he was asked at his interview. "Oh yes," he replied," I was a furniture remover in England." "How would you remove the contents of a house?" he was asked. He replied: "I would load the heavy items first and the fragile items last after protecting them with paper and such like, and if there was room carry them in the cab with me." His new employer replied: "I can see you know the system—the job's yours." The furniture removal job went very well but Scotty had this problem of being a deserter regarding his passport and paperwork, and one day he was passing a recruiting office for the Canadian Air force and saw a poster asking for ex-airmen to enlist in the reserves, especially ex-war veterans. Scotty had been a sergeant armourer in the R.A.F. during the Second World War so went into the office and told them about his R.A.F. war experiences. "You're just the type of person we are looking for!" the Officer exclaimed. At this point Scotty thought he had better come clean and explained the whole story of him deserting and being in the country illegally. The Officer told Scotty to return to the office in two days time. When Scotty returned he was apprehensive because he thought maybe immigration officials would be waiting for him, but they were not and the Officer told him he had fixed things and he would be given paperwork to legally admit him to Canada as an immigrant. A few months later, I read in the *Hull Daily Mail*, a local paper, an article reporting that Mr Scott had gone to Canada to make a new start and his family were going to join him in Canada. I haven't heard from Scotty since then but hope he and his family have made themselves a good life in Canada.

When loading in Canada we would load wheat in the holds at one port first to about halfway; then we would travel to small ports which were nothing more than saw mills to complete loading with sawn timber, where the holds were completely filled and also stacked up to about 12 feet high on the open deck, the height depending on the time of year and the stability condition of the ship. The deck cargo was then secured with chains at intervals along the deck of about 12 feet.

On one loaded voyage after we had transited the Panama Canal and were in the Caribbean Sea on our way to back to Hull, we encountered a hurricane. In the space of six hours the sea became like a boiling cauldron, the wind howling in its ferocity with mountainous waves and the ship rolling and pitching violently. It was a Sunday morning and we were in our cabin, hanging on to anything we could to keep from being thrown about, listening to a record request programme called Forces Favourites. I looked out of our cabin porthole, which faced onto the deck and a tremendous wave came over the ship's side, got under a steam-pipe guard and lifted it up as if it was nothing. The wave smashed down our alleyway door, smashed down the cabin door and before we could think, we were waist deep in seawater. I remember at the time the record requested playing on the radio was, "Why worry, why worry, worry gets you no-where at all." The Chief Officer and Carpenter appeared to make sure we were okay, and then proceeded to board up the alleyway entrance with pieces of timber in place of the door, which had gone missing. The sea, which smashed over the ship, had broken the chains and the deck cargo of timber between the amidships accommodation and our accommodation had disappeared into the sea.

These difficult sea conditions continued for the next two days but no further damage was done and it gave us time to dry out our cabin and wash our seawater-soaked clothes, not without difficulty due to the violent rolling of the ship.

Our course took us through the Caribbean Sea to the Atlantic Ocean via the Mona Passage, situated between Puerto Rico and the Dominican Republic. Due to the weather and continually overcast sky, we did not know exactly where we were but by dead reckoning position, we should have been approaching the Mona Passage. Fortunately, the sun momentarily broke through the clouds on the second mate's watch, in the afternoon, giving him just enough time to take a sight. When only one sight is taken, it does not give a position on the chart but a position line, which the ship is on. Again, fortunately, the position line was the course to steer and pass through the Mona Passage. Later, when we established our charted position, we discovered that if we had not managed to get a sight of the sun and continued on the original course we would have gone aground on the rocks south of Puerto Rica... Divine Intervention, or what?

When we arrived in the U.K. to discharge our cargo, Dougie Denman, the Chief Mate left the *Northleigh* to take a sea pilot's position from Cardiff. Another Apprentice called Arthur Harling, who was a Hull Trinity House Boy, also joined. As a replacement for Dougie Denman, Mr. Twite joined us. Mr. Twite had a charming personality but a drink problem. He had been dismissed as Master from the British Petroleum Company as a result of this problem. He was responsible for the loading and discharging of the ship and when at sea kept the 4 to 8 navigation bridge watch. That is, from 4 a.m. to 8 a.m. and 4 p.m. to 8 p.m. By this time, we were sufficiently experienced for the three Apprentices to be assigned the 4 to 8 watch, which suited our study periods with Captain Scobie.

Our next voyage was in ballast to load a full general cargo in Charleston, South Carolina in the U.S.A. The weather proved to be good on this crossing of the Atlantic. We did not have automatic steering and the ship was manually steered from the wheelhouse or in hot weather from the Monkey Island above the wheelhouse. I was on the wheel one night and Mr. Twite seemed to be in a frivolous mood. Walking across the wheelhouse, every time he took a step, he broke wind. "That's my party piece," he laughingly exclaimed as he disappeared on the wing of the bridge.

We arrived without any weather or other problems in Charleston and loaded the general cargo for Egypt. When we had finished loading and due to sail, we found that the two Assistant Stewards in the Catering Department had deserted the ship. We delayed sailing for three hours but then sailed. Captain Scobie called the Apprentices together and asked them if they would carry out the Assistant Stewards duties until we arrived in Egypt. These duties consisted of cleaning the Mates' and Engineers' cabins, bathrooms, alleyways etc., and also acting as waiters and serving meals. We would be given extra overtime at the going rate for Assistant Stewards, amounting to two shillings and sixpence (that is, about 12 and a half new pence) an hour. We grabbed the chance because it was a fortune to us and there was no refusing in any case. We divided the cleaning workload between us. I had all the amidships accommodation including cabins to clean and serve the Officers meals in the saloon.

The first day at sea after breakfast I went to clean Mr Twite, the Chief Mate's cabin. There was an awful smell in the cabin and I traced it to a clothes locker. On opening the locker the stench was overpowering and came from a pair of trousers, which had been messed. I went to Mr Twite and told him what I had found. He was not in the least embarrassed and explained, "I had an accident when I was doing my party piece on the bridge; I'll give you a couple of hours extra overtime if you wash them." "Okay," I replied without much enthusiasm. I gingerly put the offending trousers in a bucket, took them to the stern of the ship, tied a rope around them, lowered them into the sea and trailed them for about 30 minutes. When I hauled them back again on deck they had shredded to just strips of cotton. I didn't get a telling off from Mr Twite but I didn't get the couple of hours overtime either. Mr Twite was only with us for the one voyage.

With not having very much money, when in port, we always ended up at the Flying Angel or Seaman's Mission if there was one. The Mission is an organisation set up by the Anglican Church for the welfare of seafarers, where they can go to post letters, exchange books, catch up on home news through newspapers and watch films. In some of the bigger ports, they organised dances and football matches.

On one voyage, we were discharging in Rotterdam. It was February and bitterly cold. The Mission arranged a football match for us. We had a football on board the ship and thought we would get a bit of practice in. We were kicking the ball about the deck when it flew over the side into the dock water and went bobbing away in the wind. I dived into the dock and the shock of the cold water took my breath away but I managed to get the football before it disappeared, bobbing away in the distance. When I got out of the water, I couldn't speak or stop shivering but after I got under a hot shower and stayed there for 15 minutes, I was almost normal.

The next day a bus drew up at the gangway and we boarded it with our rescued football and dressed in an assortment of working shirts and boots we would be using for the match. Then off we went to pick up our opponents. We drew up outside a prison and about fourteen men, all over six feet tall, filed out of the prison gates. Two of the men were carrying a large hamper. The team turned out to be the prison warders. When we arrived at the football field, we went into separate changing rooms. We didn't need to change because we were already kitted in our working gear, so we just kicked the ball about. After about ten minutes, the prison warders trotted in line out of the changing room, just as they do at a professional football match and started kicking about. You can imagine how intimidated we felt and thought if we only lost about 20 nil we would be doing well. We had just started the match and it started snowing lightly; the warders had only scored two goals in about 10 minutes when the light snow increased to a blizzard. The football match was abandoned, much to our relief, so we adjourned to the mission for a film show instead.

We were time chartered at one part of my Apprenticeship for several voyages to West Africa, loading groundnuts, hardwood logs and cattle hides for discharge in Liverpool. The first and last port we called at in West Africa was Takoradi, Ghana, where we took on and discharged our travelling workforce of stevedores who loaded the vessel. They had their own food, cooks and their sleeping arrangement was a tarpaulin stretched between two derricks over the hatches. They were very skilled and hard workers. Their working day started at 6 a.m. and sometimes didn't finish until 10 p.m.

One problem trading on the West African coast was stowaways and we always had a thorough search for stowaways at Takoradi before we left for the U.K. On one occasion I was instructed to go into the holds and look for stowaways. A system of channels was formed in the holds utilising the sacks of groundnuts for ventilation purposes. I scrambled down a vertical channel to a horizontal channel and felt some nuts falling on my back. Looking up, there were three men lying along a box beam. I told them to go up on deck and continued my way along the horizontal channel, which opened into a large space containing fifteen more men. I told them to get back on deck and exited that area as quickly as I could. The Captain called the police who arrived and removed the stowaways in double quick time. During the voyage home to Liverpool after three days, we found another stowaway. His clothes were just rags and the crew felt sorry for him and gave him some of their own clothes.

When we arrived at Liverpool, I had to escort the stowaway to the Immigration Offices. He dressed in the clothes the crew had given him and then put his own clothes on the top of the good clothing. He looked a sight and he didn't smell very sweet. I had to use public transport, so it was a bit embarrassing for a young boy. When I presented the stowaway at the Immigration Offices, I asked the receiving Officer what would happen to the man. He said he would be detained for about ten days then sorted out with lodgings, etc. Things are certainly different nowadays.

After about three years service of my Apprenticeship we were homeward bound from America and Captain Scobie called me to his cabin. "Anderson," he said, "the third mate is leaving when we get to the U.K. and I want you to be acting third mate for the last year of your Apprenticeship. Do you want the job?" "Oh yes, *Sir,*" I answered, stressing the Sir. "Well, as part of the third mate's job he has to cut hair, so you'd better get practising." It wasn't really, but I think Captain Scobie was just trying to put me at ease and make light of the situation. However, just to be sure I practised cutting the other Apprentices hair every day until they were so bald, hair cutting made no difference. I used the haircutting skills I acquired over my entire seagoing career, even when I became a Cruise Ship Captain, as I will relate in that chapter of this book.

Thinking back, my time on the *Northleigh* passed very quickly. I made some good friends; there were plenty of interesting experiences, and I learnt lessons academic, personal and how to relate to other seamen living in a close community, which have stood me in good stead throughout my seagoing career.

So my term of Apprenticeship ended on a high note. With my Indentures completed, I was paid my laundry allowance of two pounds eight shillings, good service bonus of five pounds plus eighty-two pounds four shillings and three pence for the time I should have received Apprentice pay but was Third Mate—a total of eighty-nine pounds, twelve shillings and three pence, a small fortune in 1953.

Chapter Four

Deck Officer Years

WHEN I ARRIVED HOME after completing my Apprenticeship, I attended the Hull Trinity House Adult School to prepare myself for my Second Mate's Certificate of Competency examination. Fortunately, due to the superb tuition I had received from Captain Scobie throughout my four years service on the *Northleigh*, I did not require a very extensive period of instruction. In fact, I took the examination after only five weeks at the School and passed first time. The examination consisted of three parts, signalling, written and oral examinations.

When I was studying for my qualification as Second Mate, also my First Mate and Master's Certificates, my good friend Peter Atherton, who had been at Trinity School at the same time as me, was studying for the same qualifications; however, he attended the Hull Nautical School Adult Department and on a night, we got together and revised. It is amazing how so much better and easier it is to revise with a friend with the same interests.

After obtaining my Second Mate's Certificate of Competency, I was offered a position as Third Mate in Tatems but I decided that I should "spread my wings" and see what other Shipping Companies had to offer. I applied to a Company called Elder Dempster, who traded principally on the West Coast of Africa, had the medical and was duly accepted as a suitable person and assigned to a vessel called the *Mary Kingsley* as Third Mate.

The *Mary Kingsley* was a passenger/cargo vessel, carrying up to 12 passengers and cargo. The reason it was only 12 passengers is that if the vessel carried over 12 passengers the vessel would also be required to carry a doctor.

I joined the vessel in Liverpool on the 13th of July 1953 and signed the Articles of Agreement, which stipulate what salary and food you are entitled to in return for your service. There were two types of Agreement, A or B. Elder Dempsters used the A Agreement which meant you were paid a higher salary than the B Agreement but did not receive any overtime payments. When we arrived on the West Coast of Africa, I realised why the Company used the A Agreement—because during the discharging and loading at the different ports we worked all hours imaginable and it seemed as if Wilberforce had not got slavery abolished for people working for Elder Dempsters! I left Elder Dempsters when the *Mary Kingsley* arrived back in Liverpool on the 29th of September 1953.

On the 22nd of October 1953, I joined an oil tanker called the *Waziristan*, owned by Common Brothers of Newcastle-upon-Tyne as Third Mate and was on that ship for four voyages until the 21st March 1955.

One or two incidents stick in my mind while serving on the *Waziristan*. I took the Apprentices for studying, possibly because I had the legacy from Captain Scobie and knew the valuable input he had made to my nautical education, which they also greatly appreciated.

The Chief Mate was a drunkard and a bully and when he was in one of his drunken states he usually became obnoxious and aggressive. One night we were discharging at a port in France and he was in his usual state and was going to hit one of the Apprentices when I jumped in between them, swung round and hit the Chief Mate directly on the chin with a punch Joe Louis would have been proud of. The Mate collapsed like a sack of potatoes. The Apprentices helped me carry him to his cabin. I made sure he wasn't in any danger of choking if he vomited by placing him in the recovery position; then the Apprentices took turns watching over him in half hour periods for a couple of hours until he was sleeping like a baby. In the morning he said he couldn't recall what had happened and we didn't make him any wiser.

During the last voyage, we discharged a cargo of refined oil in Argentina at a port called La Plata. Just beyond the Oil Storage area were open fields, so when I was off duty, I went for a walk in the fields and came across some men riding bare backed horses. I asked if I could have a ride. They thought the request was hilarious and fell about laughing, but lifted me onto this thin, bony backed horse, then gave it a hard slap and it shot off like a bullet from a gun. I was bouncing up and down on this bony backed horse and the base of my spine felt as if it was being pounded with a rivet gun. After about 100 yards of this torture, I fell off the horse. The men rode up, caught the horse and laid me belly first over its back and we walked back to the end of the field. I could hardly walk and the pain at the base of my spine was excruciating but I managed to carry on my duties with some difficulty.

We received orders to proceed to Curacao, an island north of Venezuela, to load a cargo of refined oil for discharge again at La Plata, but on the way we had to divert up the Amazon River until we came to fresh water and load the fresh water from the River for Curacao because Curacao wasn't self sufficient with Fresh Water. After leaving La Plata we cleaned the cargo tanks for the reception of the fresh water and duly loaded the fresh water about 1,000 miles up the Amazon River.

On the voyage from La Plata to Curacao, I developed a cyst at the base of my spine, probably due to my horse riding antics, which was causing me continuous pain and sleepless nights but I was still carrying out my duties.

On arrival at Curacao, I visited the doctor who diagnosed a Pilonidal Sinus, which would require surgery and suggested that I be sent home for the treatment. In 1955, anyone repatriated from abroad for medical or other reasons was usually transported by a British Registered Vessel, bound for the U.K., as a Distressed British Seaman (DBS). The transporting Company could not refuse, according to the Merchant Shipping Acts, to accommodate a DBS. Arrangements were made by the British Consul for me to join a Shell Oil Tanker, which was due to sail for Glasgow. I duly arrived at the tanker and presented myself to the Captain. He seemed quite annoyed and in no uncertain terms stated that while I was on the ship I had to behave myself, not to wander around the ship and keep in my cabin out of the way as much as possible. I was a little taken aback by his attitude but people are all different so I put his attitude down to this phenomena. However, I found out another Deck Officer was being repatriated to the U.K. as a DBS but this Officer had been discharged from his ship for being a drunkard and allegedly had sabotaged the loading of an oil cargo in his vessel by mixing the grades. The Captain thought I was this second DBS and when he realised his mistake did apologise to me.

On arrival at Glasgow, the Shipping Master gave me a rail ticket to Hull plus £2 for a meal and expenses.

On arrival home I visited my doctor and was "fast tracked" to Mr Young, a specialist who performed the operation. The sinus was cut out leaving quite a large wound. The wound was packed with a dressing so that it would heal from the inside out. I understand not all pilonidal sinus operations are successful, but Mr Young did an excellent job and I've had no problems up to this day. The redressing of the wound was very painful because the old dressing was pulled out of the wound and new dressing packed in every day.

While in hospital one of the nurses attending me was an 18-year-old cracker and in her first year of training. She had long hair tied in a ponytail and quite good looking. I called her "Trigger" and she gave me the first injection she had done. When she came to give me the injection, she appeared quite nervous and said, "Where do you want it?" I didn't know I had the option where the deed was done, so replied, "I would prefer it in my thigh." She put the needle on my thigh, I tensed my muscle and she bent the needle. Attraction Chemistry must have resulted because after a long courtship she became my wife.

The future Mrs Anderson.

After recovering from my operation, I attended the Hull Trinity House School Adult Department to study for my First Mate's Certificate of Competency. After studying for six weeks, I sat the examination and passed first time again, in October 1958.

While studying for my First Mate's Certificate during the summer holiday break, my friend Peter Atherton asked me if I wanted to go and have a look around Buckingham Palace. Apparently his cousin, Terry Atherton, was training to be a footman at the Palace and relatives could go for tea and tab nabs in the servants' quarters.

Off we went down to London and stayed at his Aunt's house for a couple of days. Terry told us to go to the side entrance of the Palace where a Police Sergeant would sign us in. I'm sure the security is very much more complicated now.

We followed Terry's instructions, went to the side entrance and after a verbal cross-examination from the Police Sergeant, who had been forewarned by Terry of our impending visit (in fact Terry was waiting at the side door), he took us to the kitchen, where we had tea and tab nabs; then he took us up some stairs, which led off from the kitchen, along a corridor, which had rooms radiating from it, which apparently were storerooms. As we passed the various rooms, Terry was giving a running commentary as to the contents. "This room contains paintings, this room contains presents from various country donors," etc., etc. Then we went down some stairs into a reception area. To one side there was a big golden gong, about six feet in circumference. There was also a gleaming small red MG car. I cannot remember if it was battery or peddle power driven, which Prince Charles used. As we were looking at the contents of the reception area, a voice boomed from above: "Terence, who are your friends?" Looking up, standing on a balcony was a very distinguished looking man, immaculately dressed. "They are my cousins, sir," Terry answered, "and I'm just showing them around." "Right, give them a good tour but no photographing," the distinguished man said. Terry did tell us his name but I've forgotten. It wasn't Prince Philip because the Royal Family was not in residence at this time. I think they were at Balmoral.

Terry gave us a fantastic tour. He showed us the balcony, situated above the throne room where investitures are performed and the servants can view the proceedings behind trelliswork. We also visited the cinema room. There were a few rows of chairs. The Queen and Prince Phillip have a chair either side of a bank of telephones and various buttons. I had a sit in Prince Phillip's chair, which is or was very comfortable. I am sure there will have been alterations and refurbishments since I had this unique tour; after all, it's been all of 50 years since the tour. This was a most memorable holiday interlude between studying for my Mate's Certificate and returning to my career at sea.

After passing my examinations, I contacted Common Brothers to inform them I had obtained my Mates Certificate and wanted to sail on a general cargo ship. At that time they only had one general cargo ship and they didn't have any vacancies, but wanted me to join one of the oil tankers. I declined and joined King Line as Second Mate on a ship called the *King Alfred*. I was a year on this vessel, sailing from Liverpool to South Africa, Japan, Cuba and back to Liverpool, discharging and loading cargo in several ports of each country.

It was a pleasant experience and the only incident of note was when we came back to Liverpool. The crew were "paid off", which means they were paid their accumulated salaries less deductions incurred. The Captain had been drinking and his mind was a bit fuddled. He was seated behind a table with the Shipping Master and Agent. The crew were lined up and presented their account of wages, which had been calculated and prepared by the Captain. The Shipping Master called out the amount of cash due each seaman, and the Captain counted out the cash and gave it to the seaman who then signed the Articles of Agreement to signify he had received the payment due to him. Most of the crew had over £100 due to them and the Captain was giving them a bundle of notes secured with an elastic band as £100 and the remainder in loose notes and coin. Half way through the "Pay Off", the Captain ran out of money and told the Agent he had not received the full amount of cash but the Agent was adamant that he had given the full amount. The mystery was solved when a bundle of money paid to the last paid seaman was discovered to contain £500. The Captain in his befuddled state of mind had been handing out £500 as £100. There was then a panic to collect all the money back, but two of the seamen had already left the ship! We found out they had gone to Lime Street Railway Station to catch a train to Newcastle so I was elected to go to Lime Street and if they had not caught the train to try and persuade them to return to the ship. I arrived at the station and found them 20 minutes before the train was due to depart. I explained the situation and they agreed to return to the ship with me. They still had their pay off in bundles. When we arrived back on the ship, the situation had been resolved except for the excess cash the two seamen had. This was soon sorted out much to the relief of the Captain who had to have another drink to steady his nerves!

I did not want to continue in employment with the King Line so after a suitable period of leave, I sought employment with a Company called Curry's of Leith. Initially I joined a ship called the *Lapland* as Second Mate, which sailed from Immingham, bound for Antwerp to load a general cargo for West Africa. Fortunately, the Articles were B Agreement, so overtime was paid. The voyage lasted seven months with the discharging and loading of general cargo at several West African ports and subsequently the discharge of cargo in Hull. I left the vessel for leave on the 29th July 1957.

On the 2nd of October 1957, I joined the Curry Line's *M.V. Ireland*, a cargo/passenger vessel as Second Mate, trading from London to ports around the Mediterranean in Spain and Italy. These round trip voyages took six weeks and were most enjoyable. In fact, it was like being paid for a working holiday. I stayed on the *Ireland* until the 21st of April 1958, after which I left to attend the Hull Trinity House Adult School to study for my Master's Certificate of Competency. I attended the school for two and a half months, then took the examination and passed first time again. I decided to stay on at school to study and attempt my Extra Master's Certificate of Competency, the highest Deck Officer qualification at that time, but I ran out of cash and had to go back to sea. I rejoined the *Ireland* as Second Mate on the 12th of November 1958.

During the period between 1955, when I first met my ideal nurse and sole mate Jacqui, and 1958, I "courted" her and married her on the 26th. December 1958, while on Christmas leave from the *Ireland*. We didn't have much cash and after the Registry Office Marriage Ceremony and paying for rail tickets to London for Jacqui, we only had £8 left. My best man, Geoff Wood, provided the car transport to the Registry Office and my mum provided the reception at home. The honeymoon on my part was a working one back on the *Ireland* in London Docks, but we did manage to have a guided tour on a visit to the Tower of London and queued to view the crown jewels. We also managed to visit Madame Tussaud's to view all the waxworks depicting famous people and pay extra to view the Chamber of Horrors, which showed various people in waxwork form being tortured in a horrible manner. This was an area very popular with children, judging by the childish screams mixed with the artificially produced screams and groans coming from the chamber.

I remained on the *Ireland* until June 1959, when I realised there was no prospect of further promotion in the Company due to the sale of some of Curry's ships. I then re-applied for employment to Common Brothers of Newcastle who appointed me as Second Mate on the *Border Lass*, a product oil tanker, which I joined in August 1959.

Between this interim period on leave, our son Carl John was born on July the 12th 1959, a birthday present for Jacqui because she was born on July the 12th as well, but in 1936. We lived with Jacqui's parents on North Hull Estate because we couldn't afford to be buying a house at that time. Carl was the apple of both grandparents' eyes and spoilt. He was a lovely, blond, well-behaved baby and always laughing. Isn't it strange how they change when they reach their teens?

The Captain on the *Border Lass* was named Willy Fairley and was Second Mate when I was Third Mate on the *Waziristan*. We were already friends so it was fortunate that I was assigned the *Border Lass* for my first ship, which proved to be a long association with Common Brothers.

I was promoted to Chief Mate on the *Border Sentinel*, another Oil Tanker in July 1960, and served on various ships owned or managed by Messrs Common Brothers in that capacity until I was promoted to Captain in May 1963.

On the 25th of February 1962, I was First Mate on a ship named the *Border Keep* and we were anchored off the Humber, waiting to berth at Salt End in Hull. Jacqui was due to give birth to our second child and Captain Bedigan, the Master, gave me permission to get a lift from the pilot boat and attend the birth. When I arrived at my in-laws, Jacqui was in labour at the nursing home. I phoned the nursing home, asked how she was and was informed that she had had the baby, and that baby and mum were doing well. I said I'd be right there and went to tell my in-laws the good news. "What did Jacqui have?" I was asked. "I don't know," I replied. So I went back to the public phone box to ring and ask. "It's a girl," I was told. I duly reported back to the in-laws, then went to see our baby daughter, Susan, who had black hair, a wrinkled face and screamed when she saw me. She cried most of the time.

By this time I could afford to put the deposit down on a house and we moved into a two bedroomed house, which cost £1, 800.

During the time I was Chief Mate, I had served with several Captains. Most were what you would call normal, but a couple of them had peculiar idiosyncrasies. One of them we nicknamed Prudence because he always wrote in his letters to the office, "I thought it prudent to reduce speed to arrive at the port in daylight." *Prudent* was his favourite word whatever the reason. He often gave a piano recital, using the chart table as his imaginary piano. I think he must have been a brilliant pianist because he made the noise of the piano notes with his mouth and was always note perfect. During the recital he was prone to give any observers sideways coy looks and flutter his eyelashes!

Another Captain called "Tex" Bedigan, who I admired very much, had failed his driving test several times and had a car driving control facsimile, including gear lever, clutch, brake, accelerator pedals and steering wheel set up in his bathroom and would practice seated on his toilet seat, making the gear changes with his hands and feet and vocally producing the appropriate sounds associated with gear changes. He would ask me to observe his driving skills and give orders for an emergency stop and on my command would plant both feet firmly on the brake and clutch, accompanying this action with a suitable noise effect with his mouth, a high, ear-piecing screech. I had to give him a fail or pass.

When we returned to the U.K. and dry-docked, Tex went for his driving test and passed. He told me that his emergency stop was excellent except without thinking he also gave the vocal similarity, which rather unsettled the examiner, who passed him anyway.

Tex had been a prisoner of war in Germany. In 1940, Tex was an Apprentice on a ship loading in Narvik, Norway. He had gone to bed at night and when he woke up in the morning the quay was full of German soldiers. He shot off to wake the mate up, who wouldn't believe his story about the German Soldiers being on the quay, but at that moment a loudspeaker blasted a message in English for everyone to come out on deck. The crew were gathered together, told to collect their belongings, given an armed guard and escorted to the border between Sweden and Norway, where they were handed over to Swedish authorities. They were put into an internment camp and worked on various farms in the surrounding area.

This went on for about six months and Tex said it was great, good food, good company; the Swedish people were very supportive and things couldn't have been better, taking into account the circumstances. Then he made the biggest mistake of his life. An Official from England visited the camp and asked for volunteers to man a British ship, which had been detained in Stockholm but now had orders to leave the country. Tex was one of the volunteers and they were transported to Stockholm. Apparently, they had to leave by a certain day and everything had to be very secretive and hush hush. The Britsh Meteorological Department were involved to forecast when it would be suitably foggy so that the visibility would be reduced and the ship have less chance of being spotted by German Warships when they cleared Swedish Territorial Waters and avoid capture. The fog forecast was made and the British Ship made ready to sail. On sailing day, the ship was to sail at 6 a.m. As occasionally is the case, even today, on this day, when everything was dependent on a correct forecast, the Meteorological Department had got the forecast wrong. The day broke fine, not a cloud in the sky. Visibility about 30 miles and as for the secrecy, when they sailed from Stockholm to the open sea, all the way was lined with spectators wanting to give them a good send off. Needless to say, as soon as they cleared Swedish Territorial Waters, the German Warships appeared; the crew were captured and sent to a Prisoner of War Camp in Germany. Tex ended up with one of the better jobs; he was assisting in the disposal of garbage outside the camp area near a farm, so was able to barter with the farmers for eggs and vegetables in exchange for Red Cross parcels.

While in the camp Tex studied for his Second Mate's Certificate and sat the exam at the end of the war.

As I stated in the forward of this book, everyone should write down their life experiences. I don't know if Tex did, but his experiences are unique and would have been a good subject matter for a Film or TV Series.

I have learnt a precious lesson sailing with different Captains, some good things and some things to avoid at all costs. Most were gentlemen but one or two were obnoxious drunkards. During my time as a Ship's Captain on all types of vessels, I have tried to apply the knowledge obtained from the different experiences. "That is what life is all about!"

Chapter Five

Cargo Ship Captain Years

O N THE 3RD OF MAY 1963, I was Chief Officer on an Iron Ore Vessel called the *Dagestan* and was told to proceed home on leave for a couple of weeks. After about a week at home, I received a phone call from the Company informing me that I had been promoted to Master and was to join an Oil Tanker called the *Border Sentinel* in Abadan, Iran, as Master. The full impact of this news did not register until I had completed the phone call; then a feeling of elation overcame me and I think Jacqui and I had a little impromptu dance to celebrate. I was 29 years old at the time, quite young to be promoted to Master.

In those days, seamen could travel on their Seaman's Discharge Book in lieu of a passport and I did not give any thought to obtaining a visa. I flew by Comet from Heathrow to Abadan, arriving at night. Our British Agent in the airport, who was a little bit under the weather from drink, met me. When I came to go through Immigration, they would not allow me to land because I did not have a visa. The Agent was a bit loud and staggering around. "I'll take care of it," he said and pulled out a roll of banknotes to bribe the Immigration Officer with, in full view of everyone around. I was refused entry and had to reboard the aircraft and go on to Bombay, where our agent in Bombay met me. I obtained the necessary visa from the Iranian Consul and returned by the same plane to Abadan, where the same Agent met me, fully sober and very sheepish. I duly joined the *Border Sentinel*, which had been delayed three hours waiting for me. All the vessel's documents were handed over to me and we sailed for East Africa. It was a somewhat inauspicious beginning to my career as Ship's Captain.

Common Brothers by this time owned or managed about 32 vessels of all types, Oil Tankers, Iron Ore Carriers, General Cargo Vessels, Freezer Vessels and Container Vessels. Later, they also owned Roll On-Roll Off container vessels and were probably one of the first shipping companies to operate in this type of trade. I served as Captain on most of them during my time as Master with Common Brothers and there were experiences I was subjected to and will relate, which I am sure will interest any readers of this book.

In 1965 I was appointed Captain to a ship called the *Iron Barque*, an Iron Ore Carrier, which was in Glasgow and due to sail for Murmansk, USSR, to load a cargo of Iron Ore. At that time the "Cold War" was on and if any ships went to the USSR the Master had to land their secret coded documents before sailing; also, if any of the crew were Latvians or Estonians who had settled in Britain, they were discharged from the vessel, in case, when they arrived in the USSR, they were detained. Before sailing, we were visited by two MI5 Agents. The crew were gathered in the smoke room, where the Agents showed silhouettes of Russian War Ships. Members of the crew were asked to covertly take photographs on the way to Murmansk if they sighted any of the illustrated War Ships and report back. When the MI5 Agents departed, I told the crew to do nothing of the kind because if they were caught they would certainly be sent to Siberia or worse and they could not expect to get any help from the British Government.

Off we sailed. Murmansk is in the Arctic Circle and the temperature is constantly below freezing, but due to the Gulf Stream going over the North Cape it remains navigable and the river ice-free. At that time, the Russian People living there were paid bonuses to attract workers and compensate for the weather conditions. We arrived at the River entrance to Murmansk and the Russian Pilot boarded. He could speak excellent English and was quite a pleasant man. On the way upriver, we passed plenty of War Ships tied up and I was hoping the crew were following my instructions and not taking any photographs.

When we had docked, armed guards were posted around the ship. After signing the necessary papers and documents, the pilot who was acting as translator for the port officials said, "Have you been to Murmansk before?" "No," I replied. "Well, tonight I'll take you for a nice fish meal and show you around. I'll meet you at the dock gate at 6 p.m. because I cannot come into the docks after six," he stated.

At 6 p.m. sharp, I showed my pass at the dock gate and was greeted outside by the pilot. "First of all, I want to show you our new department store," he said in a proud manner. He took me to this single story, long wooden hut. We entered and there were shelves with nothing on them. At the end of the store was a jumbled heap of fur boots tied together, alongside a rack of fur hats. There was also a pile of second-hand 78 gramophone records and he insisted on buying me a record of Tchaikovsky's 1812 Overture. After leaving the department store, we went for a meal. The restaurant was situated inside the main railway station. We approached the restaurant via a long corridor with an equally long queue of people waiting for a table. I stopped at the end of the queue to wait our turn but the pilot said, "Come on," and continued walking to the head of the queue. A very large commissionaire in full uniform stood by a door from which the full expanse of the restaurant could be seen. The pilot said something to him in Russian and the commissionaire's attitude abruptly changed; he stood to attention, gave me a salute and disappeared into the restaurant. He went to a table with six people on it, four soldiers and two civilians who had been served and were eating their meal. He spoke sharply to the two civilians who immediately left their half eaten meal and vacated their chairs. The plates were cleared away and much to my embarrassment, we were shown to the vacated seats.

The soldiers at the table were Officers and showed a great interest in me. They engaged the pilot in a lengthy conversation. When I asked the pilot what they were saying, he said, "They just want to know who you are and what nationality. I told them to mind their own business or they would find themselves in the salt mines in Siberia." I'm sure he was just joking because they were just smiling and nodding their heads at me.

The pilot ordered our meal and it seemed as if all the meals were fish meals, cooked the way you wanted them. While we were waiting for our meal, the Officers held a conversation with me through the pilot and insisted on giving me a small glassful of Vodka, which I had to down in one go. The Officer seated next to me was a Doctor and noticed my watch, which was an Omega Seamaster, a quite expensive watch. He took off his watch, which was a scruffy stained watch and a MUMF make. He gestured and held out his watch. "What does he want?" I asked the pilot. The pilot said, "In Russia, as a sign of friendship, people exchange watches—but don't pay any attention to him."

The meal took some time arriving and the Officers were taking it in turn to fill my glass with vodka, which I always had to down in one go. By the time the meal arrived, I could hardly speak never mind eat. I didn't remember finishing my meal or anything else until I woke up inside the dock area, collapsed in the snow. I was extremely cold and think my Guardian Angel must have been looking after me because I'm sure I would have frozen to death. The Vodka must have also helped to keep me alive. Somehow I managed to stagger back to the ship and the guard must have helped me to my cabin, where I must have collapsed in my bed, although I don't remember anything between having started my meal in the restaurant and waking up in my own bed on the ship. I woke up with a start, looked a my watch to see the time and my watch had mysteriously changed from an Omega Seamaster to a Russian MUMF which seemed to have stopped keeping time. It must have broken when I fell inside the dock area—or it may have been already broken. On my table was a broken gramophone record, so I must have broken that when I fell down in the dock area.

We completed loading Iron Ore that day and the same pilot came to take us out to sea. I asked him about the watch. He said I was in such a drunken state the doctor had insisted on changing watches as an act of friendship and after the meal, the pilot with the help of the Officers had helped me to the control point in the docks and sent me on my way back to the ship.

The moral to this story is, if you visit Russia don't wear an expensive watch and don't accept unlimited tots of Vodka from Russian Army Officers.

By 1966, the Company had given permission for Senior Officers to be accompanied on voyages by their wives and children, so in January 1966 I took advantage of the Company's generosity and my wife Jacqui, son Carl who was 6 and daughter Susan who was 3 joined the *Iron Barque* in Swansea for a six-month period. Jacqui had to get permission from the education authority for Carl to take the voyage. She was given six months of lessons to teach him and instructed to keep the resulting papers as proof of the lessons he had completed.

Off we sailed in ballast towards Pointe-Noire in the Congo to load iron ore. Crossing the Bay of Biscay heading South Westerly we encountered a South Westerly gale. The seas were very high, making the ship pitch, pound, and roll violently with seas breaking over the ship's bow. The windows of my accommodation faced the foredeck, directly beneath the bridge, so I had a good view of the horizon and the foredeck of the ship. Carl was in a chair propped against a bulkhead so that he could look out of the window. It was rather exciting for a six-year-old and he shouted, "Make it do it again dad, make it do it again!" Ten minutes later he was feeling seasick, lying down on the carpet and saying, "Am I dying dad? Will I go to heaven?"

The bad weather lasted for about two days before the seas calmed. The sun shone and the air temperature started to increase as we progressed southwards and life was all rosy again.

The weather became rather warm so the Engineers prefabricated a swimming pool between No.1 and No.2 hatches with wooden planks and canvas tarpaulins. The Second Engineer, Stan Carr, who had a lovely way with children and adults for that matter, taught Carl and Susan to swim.

When we crossed the equator, Neptune appeared on board, looking very much like the Second Mate in disguise, accompanied by his entourage of Aphrodite, Photographer, Doctor, Barber and numerous Policemen, all looking very similar to various members of the crew.

Neptune's policemen collected those crewmembers that had not crossed the Equator before, including Jacqui, Carl and Susan. They were all given a rough initiation ceremony, which included a black grease shampoo by the barber (Stan Carr) and a large gob-stopper soap pill by the doctor (Chief Steward), followed by a ducking in the improvised swimming pool. All these activities were being recorded on film by Neptune's Official Photographer who happened to be the Chief Engineer.

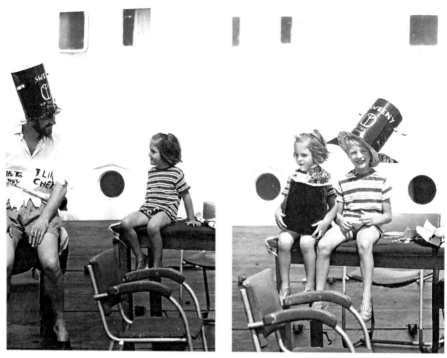

Stan Carr talking to daughter, Susan after the ceremony.

Son Carl & daughter Susan after the ceremony.

Jacqui had the rough treatment but Carl and Susan were treated very gently and instead of the gob-stopper soap pill, they received a sweet and were lowered gently into the swimming pool. I had a surprise at the end of the ceremony of those who had been done, because the policemen grabbed me and subjected me to the roughest treatment of all, even though I had previously crossed the equator.

Jacqui getting the treatment.   Me getting the very rough treatment.

All the people "done" were given a certificate so that they could show they had partaken in the crossing the line ceremony and wouldn't be subjected to the initiation ceremony again.

This is to certify that JACQUELINE MARGARET ANDERSON, on the 23rd. day of March in the year 1966, aboard the M.V. " IRON BARQUE ", did pay tribute in the recognised manner on the occasion of CROSSING THE EQUATOR, thereby acknowledging our royal personages, sovereignty of the SEVEN SEAS and ASSOCIATED WATERS, by which act she is entitled to all priviliges and immunities subject to the observance of our laws.

WITNESS TO THE SIGNATURE OF NEPTUNIS REX

.... Amphodrite
.... Clark of the Court
.... Doctor
.... Barber
.... Policeman

Neptunis Rex.

Jacqui's crossing the line certificate.

We eventually arrived at Pointe-Noire and loaded a cargo of Iron Ore to be discharged at Dunkerque, in France. After discharging in Dunkerque, we received orders to proceed to Sept Iles (Seven Islands) in Canada to load a Cargo of Iron Ore for Glasgow. During the sea passage towards Sept Iles Susan had her 4th Birthday and the crew prepared a surprise birthday party for her, complete with a cake, presents and hand-made birthday cards. Seamen are a bit soft when it comes to young kids and I'm sure whatever ship they are on they are made a fuss of and spoilt.

Nearing Newfoundland and in the Gulf of Saint Lawrence, we encountered Icebergs which excited the children.

After loading in Sept Iles, we proceeded to Glasgow for discharge. On arrival in Glasgow Jacqui and the children left the ship.

During the time on the ship, Jacqui had religiously given Carl the lessons as designated by the Education Authorities, with the added benefits of real life geography lessons. When Carl returned to school, he was actually way beyond the standard of his class and had to mark time in his school lessons, which held him back from progressing at the rate he was making.

In 1968 the Company started building Roll On/Roll Off Container Vessels, specifically for the Caribbean Trade. As I was going to be appointed Master of the first vessel, I attended and helped supervise the building, in a Builders' Yard called Sietas of Blankanese on the River Elbe in Germany. The ship was built in a dry-dock and the launching was a simple process: the dock was just flooded and the ship floated out. The ship was named the *Caribbean Venture*. My wife Jacqui attended the ceremony with me and the builders provided the usual launching celebratory meal afterwards.

The ship sailed in ballast from Germany to Miami, Florida, which was going to be our main cargo loading/discharging operations port to Venezuela. On arrival at Miami, we had an open day when the Mayor, shippers and interested people were given a tour of the ship with drinks and eats on completion of the tour. The concept of a Roll On/Roll Off vessel trading to Venezuela created lots of interest with shippers because the cargo, secured in containers, eliminated pilfering of cargo, which was rife; and also, the cargo designated to various towns could be driven directly from the ship with no cargo handling at the port.

We loaded a full cargo of containers on lorry chasses and sailed for La Guaira, Venezuela. We had been scheduled to arrive and take on board the sea pilot at 6 a.m. However, on arrival at the pilot station, there was no sign of him. I steamed around the pilot station until 11 a.m. when he belatedly arrived and boarded us. He came on the navigation bridge and handed me a letter from the ship's Owner, Sandy Common. It read: 'We are having some problems with the stevedores. All the ports in Venezuela have sent representatives to demonstrate against the use of Roll On/Roll Off vessels.

There are about 5,000 demonstrators. On arrival at the berth, instruct your men to be mindful of missiles and on no account throw anything back.' We proceeded to the discharge berth and were greeted by a host of banner-waving protesters, men, women and children. When the mooring ropes were put on the shore bollards, they were immediately thrown off and we could not be secured to the dock. After about 30 minutes, three or four army transport trucks arrived and armed soldiers pushed the demonstrators away from the quay so that we could be moored. The Dockers immediately put two mobile cranes across the stern door of the vessel to prevent any discharging of cargo. A few missiles had been thrown but no harm done. The noise and chanting was deafening. On a level with the navigation bridge on the quay was a ramp with about 100 people on it who were shouting slogans, but we just smiled and waved to them. After a while, the intimidating atmosphere seemed to change into a carnival atmosphere and the demonstrators were returning our smiles and waves.

Sandy Common boarded the vessel and told me the situation was very tense and he was in negotiations with the local authorities and the stevedores union. We would have to wait and see if the negotiations were successful.

The next day, it appeared as if the situation had deteriorated, with the likelihood of violence, so Sandy went on radio and television to announce the vessel would be leaving La Guaira that afternoon to prevent any further problems and possible violence.

When we sailed from La Guaira, the protestors attended in greater numbers than when we had arrived and it was a real carnival atmosphere with drums, trumpets, etc., to accompany the singing.

We returned to Miami to await further orders until a decision had been made as to the future trading area we would have to establish. Life became a pleasant routine for about ten days, and then things abruptly changed in a disastrous manner.

I was having a pre-lunchtime drink with the Ship's Agent in a restaurant when the bar telephone rang. The barman answered and shouted out, as they do, "Is there anyone here called Captain Anderson?" I indicated I was that person and he handed me the telephone. It was the Chief Officer. "There has been an explosion in the engine room and water is pouring in!" he shouted as if I was deaf, which I wasn't—well, not at that time. "Have you closed the Engine room Watertight Doors?" I enquired." "Yes," he answered. "Okay," I acknowledged, "I'm on my way back." The Agent drove me back to the ship in record time and there were all kinds of activity at the berth—Miami Emergency Services, Police, the Fire Service, Coast Guard, Newspaper Reporters, even lawyers, ready to ply their trade if anyone was injured. Word must have spread like a forest fire.

I went on board the ship to be greeted by the Chief Officer and a Coast Guard Officer who was holding a sample bottle containing oil and water. "I'm afraid I'm going to have to hold you responsible for polluting the harbour," he stated, holding the bottle up as evidence. Needless to say, that was the least of my worries.

In the company of the Chief Engineer and Chief Officer, I proceeded to the top of the Engine room and viewed the scene. Water ingress into the Engine room had stopped. The engines and auxiliary machinery had been completely submerged by the seawater topped by a covering of fuel oil.

The act of closing the Engine room watertight doors had contained the water ingress to the main engine room and had saved the ship from sinking and settling on the seabed. At least we were still afloat.

Fortunately, the explosion happened at lunchtime and there was only one person on watch in the engine room, for the rest were having their lunch. The person on watch in the engine room was a donkey man and he had been quite a distance from the area of the explosion; in fact, he was near the ladders leading up to the deck. He told me that by the time he had started going up the ladders, he was up to his waist in oil and seawater and he was still shocked.

When I went back on deck, the Agent handed me a letter. "Oh, by the way, this letter has been in the Office for a couple of days but I forgot to bring it to you," he said sheepishly. The letter was from the British Consul addressed to me and stated that the F.B.I. had advised him to inform all British Registered Vessels that they had obtained information an Anti-Castro Cuban Organisation was going to plant a bomb on a British Vessel which was berthed in the port of Miami. This act was because Britain was trading with Cuba and the Anti-Castro Organisation was trying to discourage the British Government from trading with Cuba.

I telephoned the Company to relate the disastrous news and Foster Davison, one of our Superintendents, was dispatched post haste to review the situation and arrange salvage agreements with a local salvage company. Meanwhile, as there was no lighting or air-conditioning or any services for that matter due to having the generators submerged in seawater, I accommodated the crew in a hotel, except for myself and chief engineer. We stayed on the ship for security reasons.

The bombing was reported in the *Miami Herald* and two days later, an open letter was published by them from the Anti-Castro Organisation, who stated, that they were sorry for the harbour pollution but the bomb was supposed to have exploded while the vessel was at sea.

Our Superintendent, Foster Davison, had arranged for a salvage company to attend, and make the ship watertight so that we could be towed to Jacksonville, Florida, for sufficient repairs so that we could be towed back to Germany for permanent repairs.

We had a meeting with the working boss of the salvage company as to how they were going to effect repairs sufficient for the vessel to be towed to Jacksonville. He was dressed like a cowboy, Stetson hat, jeans, checked shirt and high-heeled boots, without the spurs. He was continually chewing a large cigar and I never did see him light it. He didn't give us much confidence but looks can be deceiving and in this case, they were because he accomplished everything he said he would do.

Foster asked him how he was going to make the ship watertight to be towed to Jacksonville for temporary repairs. "Well," the boss replied in a deep Southern drawl, which I found quite attractive, "first of all, I'm going to dive and inspect the size of the hole I'm going to cover. Then I'm going to cover the hole with seven eights marine plywood. I secure the plywood to the hull by shooting steel bolts through the plywood and steel hull and go around the edges of the plywood with quick drying cement, especially formulated for application in seawater to make a watertight joint. Then I'm going to pump out the contaminated water from the engine room into my salvage barge. When the engine room is dry, I'm going to fill the hole completely with cement and added steel bars for strengthening. Then you'll be ready to go!"

Foster exchanged dubious glances with me and said to the boss, "Are you sure seven eights marine ply will be strong enough to do the trick? There will be a terrific pressure on the plywood when you pump the water out of the engine room."

"Listen you guys," the boss drawled in a condescending manner, as if he was talking to school kids, "this aint going to fail, I'll stake my life on it. I've got my reputation to think about. I've got my scuba gear with me and a spare set— do you want to come down with me Captain and have a look at the damage?"

"I've never been Scuba diving before," I told him.

"Have you ever had a suck on a ladies titty?" he said. I suppose that is what Texans call a lady's breast.

"Well, occasionally, but not for some time," I replied.

"Just do that with the Scuba mouthpiece and you won't go wrong. Keep near me and I'll see you won't come to any harm," he instructed.

We got changed into the Scuba gear. I had a little practice under the tuition of the Boss, remembering his operating instructions and then went onto the quay. We entered the water via a ladder. The visibility wasn't so good but I kept in close contact with the Boss as we went down the side of the ship and along the bottom towards the middle. We had about a four-foot clearance between the bottom of the ship and seabed. At that time, I realised if we hadn't closed the engine room watertight doors and contained the ingress of water to the engine room, we may have been sitting on the seabed and the salvage operations would have been complicated. We came upon a large hole in the hull, about six feet square. The ragged edges of the steel plates were bent inwards, indicating an external explosion. We found out later that the anti-Castro Cubans had secured a time bomb to the grid of the main seawater suction opening, the bomb timed to go off when the vessel was at sea.

The salvage operations went like clockwork just as the Boss said it would. When the engine room had been pumped out, I went through the surrounding area of double bottom tanks to assess the resulting damage in the vicinity of the explosion to draw up a dry-docking list of repairs, which would be needed when we finally arrived in Germany. It took about two weeks to complete the work of making the ship watertight and safe to tow to Jacksonville.

Me & Foster Davison inspecting the bomb damage after the engine
room had been pumped dry.

A Dutch Salvage Tug towed us from Miami to Jacksonville. The ship was dry-docked and the damaged bottom area cut out, the cement block dropped out, and the resulting large area steel plated over for the towed trip back to the builder's yard in Germany.

The same salvage tug towed us back across the Atlantic Ocean to the Sietas Yard on the River Elbe in Germany where the ship was built. Hull repairs and the replacement of main and auxiliary engines took about three months and then we returned to Miami to continue trading between Miami, Honduras and Guatemala, on charter to the Caribbean Trailer Express Company of Miami.

The round voyage was a weekly schedule and we employed a local Ship Chandler to buy our food and supplies, which he delivered every time we arrived in Miami. We had a total crew of 21 so the food costs were quite high. After a couple of voyages, comparing prices between Supermarkets and the Ship Chandler, it was obvious the Ship Chandler was charging us over double the food costs for his delivery services. When I was on the telephone to Common Brothers in Newcastle, giving them my weekly voyage report, I asked them if it would be okay to purchase the food requirements myself. They said as I was the Captain, I could do what I liked but to keep the feeding costs below £1.00 (2.40 Dollars) per person per day, so every time in Miami I borrowed the Charterer's truck and went shopping to the local Supermarket accompanied by the Chief Steward and Third Mate. After a couple of visits, we became well known to the Supermarket personnel. The Manager informed us regarding items on offer, such as legs of lamb, ham and extra special offers. When we had finished shopping we had at least eight stacked trolleys of food. It helped when the Manager delegated a couple of his workforce to assist us. The checkout girls always begged us to come to their checkout; I think they had a competition going on as to who took the most money in their shift. Our average weekly costs at the Supermarket were 500 Dollars, which, besides the food, also included cleaning materials, etc. The feeding costs were well under the stipulated daily allowance so we occasionally introduced a few luxuries like lobster and dinner wine.

We never bought fish because on our schedule, the first port after leaving Miami was Puerto Cortes in Honduras and we had to adjust our speed to arrive 6 a.m. on a Tuesday morning. We would arrive just off Puerto Cortes at midnight, where there was a great fishing bank with grouper, red snapper and other fish in quantity. The crew would be ready, baited up with their fishing rods and as we drifted over the bank, it was all systems go. We caught more than enough fish to last us a week, which we immediately gutted and stored in the deep-freezer.

Another advantage of shopping at the Supermarket was that we received Green Shield Stamps, the number depending on the amount of money we had spent. The Stamps could be redeemed for various merchandise such as a Film Projector, TV's, Cameras, Cine Cameras, Luxury Luggage etc. We filled a couple of books each week with the stamps and when I was relieved by the relief Captain to proceed on leave, we only had four more books of stamps to collect and then we could have redeemed the stamps for a Film Projector to have weekly films in the crew mess room. I told the relief Captain about our plan and we only needed four more books full of Green Shield Stamps to reach our objective. I went home on leave and later was informed that the relief Captain and the Third Mate had redeemed the Green Shied Stamps for Cameras and Luxury Luggage for themselves. Fortunately, I met the relief

Captain again at the Annual Company Dinner in Newcastle so was able to confront him and inform the people in the immediate area what a poor example of a human being he was, but in stronger terms.

In 1971 I was Captain of the *M.V. Caribbean Progress* on the weekly schedule Miami, Puerto Cortes, Honduras and Puerto Barrias, Guatemala, back to Miami. Due to the USA's space programme, many offshoots of the scientific discoveries were being marketed, not least of all calculators. Initially, these calculators, even the simple function type, were relatively expensive and quite bulky compared to the present day ones. Every Saturday when in Miami I received the local paper, the *Miami Herald,* from our Agent. Besides catching up on the local and worldwide news, I would scan through the advertisements to see if there were any local shop bargains. I noted on one occasion, an electrical shop on Flagler Street. For those readers who know Flagler Street, it was halfway down on the left-hand side, advertising "The affordable Calculator, 240 Dollars (equivalent then to £100), with the basic functions of add, subtract, divide and multiply, the case no bigger than a pack of cards and power supplied by a rechargeable battery, the battery charger included in the price."

As part of my duties I had all the ship's accounts to do, so this offer sounded as if it would be a good investment to reduce the mental work.

Off I went to the shop and was served by a very attentive, pleasant, smiling shop assistant. He was about 6 feet 3 inches tall, built similar to an American Football Team Blocker, and when he wasn't smiling his looks were quite intimidating—a broken nose and cruel looking eyes. I think he was aware of the projection he gave because he endeavoured to keep smiling all the time. However I had no complaints regarding the service. He showed and demonstrated the calculator and battery charger, then gift-wrapped it for me.

Halfway through the following voyage, after three days use, the battery charger malfunctioned and so the calculator was of no further use until I obtained a replacement.

On arrival back in Miami, I took my battery charger back to the shop and was greeted by the same attentive, pleasant, smiling shop assistant. "Hi, how's the calculator going?" he cheerfully enquired. Obviously, he had recognised me, probably because he didn't get many British people as customers. I showed him the battery charger, explained it wasn't working and could he give me a replacement? His manner changed from the pleasant, smiling assistant to an intimidating, aggressive, keep-your-distance approach, which, I must admit, suited his character much better.

"We don't keep spares here, you will have to send it back to Texas Instruments, sorry, can't help you," he forcefully stated.

I explained I was only in Miami for one day every week and added that if I had made the purchase in England, I could have obtained a replacement battery charger without any difficulty, to which he made the obvious retort, "Well buddy, you're in the States now and things are different here."

Another customer came into the shop, and the assistant put on his pleasant, smiling face approach and went off to serve him, more or less indicating my problems and I were history.

I was left feeling frustrated and annoyed that I was unable to change the now useless battery charger. There must be some way of making the shop assistant give me an exchange, I thought... Subconsciously I could hear the shop assistant giving the new customer his sales patter about how wonderful the calculators were and then it suddenly struck me.... *That's* the way to do it!

I walked up to the new customer and explained that I had bought a calculator the previous week, and that the battery charger was faulty and the assistant wouldn't change it for me. If that was the service given by the shop it wasn't a good idea to buy his calculator from here, and for good measure I informed him that he could get the same type of calculator cheaper at a shop further down the street.

The prospective customer thanked me for the information, murmured a few words of commiseration, looked at the shop assistant, whose Jekyll and Hyde character showed through again, and left the shop in double quick time.

"Listen bud, beat it," the assistant snarled.

At that moment, another customer came into the shop, looking at the display of calculators. The assistant adopted his smooth Dr Jekyll character and went smiling pleasantly over to the customer.

Before the assistant could begin his sales patter, I sidled up to the customer and asked him if he was going to buy a calculator, to which question he confirmed that he was. I again related my tear-wrenching story regarding the battery charger and added the same information I had given the first customer, that he could get the calculator cheaper at a shop further down the street. The last piece of information did the trick and with a murmur of thanks, he beat a hasty retreat.

The shop assistant could hardly contain himself! Coming from behind the counter with a threatening attitude, he bent and thrust his face about two inches from my face in a most ferocious manner and told me his patience had snapped and he was going to telephone the local police precinct and have his friend Detective Sergeant Macdonald come and sort me out.

The assistant went over to the telephone. I saw him lift the handset and put a finger over the rest to stop the dialled number going through, dialled a number, waited about ten seconds and commenced talking to himself.

"Is Mac there?" he enquired, "Good, can I talk to him?" He put his hand over the mouthpiece of the phone. "You had better make yourself scarce," he exclaimed to me, then took his hand from the mouthpiece. "Hello there, Mac," he said into the phone, "I've got a guy here causing problems. Can you come and sort him out?" He paused, as if listening to the other end's conversation. "Good, you'll be down in two or three minutes, fine, thanks Mac." Replacing the phone on its cradle, he said, "Okay, that's it, I've given you enough chances—you've two minutes to clear off!"

"You haven't been making a call," I said. "You had your fingers over the rest when you dialled and you've just been talking to yourself. That performance deserves an Oscar."

Adopting what I hoped appeared a reasoning and appealing manner, I said, "Look, all I want is a replacement battery charger. You can return the old one and get a refund much more easily than I can."

At that moment, a new customer entered the shop. The assistant looked at the customer, then me. I raised my eyebrows in a quizzical manner, more or less indicating I was going to foil another potential sale.

The assistant must have thought maybe an exchange was better than this crazy Limey, so he took me aside, thrust a box containing a battery charger into my hand and said, "Okay, you win—now clear off!"

"Would you mind testing it?" I enquired. "It may not work."

The assistant nearly exploded. He went red-faced, his eyes bulged, and, in fact, I thought he was having a heart attack. He didn't say a word, but with ill grace, snatched the box from my hand, tested the charger (which was okay) and thrust it back into my hand.

"Thanks," I graciously said. "Have a nice day"—and left the shop without any remarks from the shop assistant for me to have a nice day.

The battery charger worked very well and about a month later I passed the shop and the same assistant happened to be looking out. I gave him a cheerful wave and without a doubt, he recognised me because he gave me a two-fingered salute in return.

An interesting sequel to the bombing of the *Caribbean Venture* incident by the Anti-Castro Cubans in 1968 at Miami happened about four years later when I was on a ship called the *Caribbean Endeavour* trading in the same area as the *Venture*. The *Endeavour* was a much larger vessel than the *Venture* and we could accommodate four passengers. The vessel was trading on a weekly schedule from Miami to Honduras and Guatemala back to Miami. One voyage, a Cuban passenger, joined in Miami for the round voyage. He was the superintendent of a shipping company based in Miami and was going to Guatemala, where one of his company's vessels had engine problems and he was going to make personal arrangements with a local Guatemalan Repair Company regarding cost, time and repairs.

Mr Fernandes, the Cuban person, had defected from Cuba and was one of the top Cuban Dissidents wanted by Castro. He never travelled by air in case the aeroplane was highjacked and diverted to Cuba, which was happening at that time, so he always travelled by sea.

During the week he was a passenger on the *Endeavour*, we became good friends, and in the course of various conversations I told him about the bombing of the *Venture*, and he told me about his escape from Cuba.

Apparently, he had been a pilot in a fighter plane and during some manoeuvres had taken the opportunity to defect to Miami.

During one conversation he asked me if I liked Cuban food. "I've never had real Cuban food," I replied. "Well, when we get back to Miami I'll take you for lunch," he stated.

We arrived in Miami early morning and at lunchtime Mr Fernades came to pick me up and took me to a restaurant in the Cuban Quarter. On arrival he escorted me to a large table where there were five other Cuban Americans sitting. He introduced me as the Captain of the *Endeavour*, and then we ordered drinks and our meal. The waiters were very attentive and the group at the table seemed to be specially catered for. While we waited for our meal, I was introduced to a game where the last two numbers on a dollar bill produced by each person was compared and the winner collected all the contestants' dollars. The game, drinks, meal and conversation produced a very congenial atmosphere and during this period, Mr Fernandes remarked to one of the men who everyone appeared to revere, "This is the Captain who was Captain of the *Caribbean Venture* when it was blown up!" The man looked at me and said, "If I had known you then I wouldn't have done it!"

I was a bit gob-smacked and open mouthed at this statement, took a large mouthful of my gin and tonic and just said, "Thank you very much, I wish you had known me then as well!" I understand he was apprehended some years later for his activities and received a short prison sentence.

In 1974, I was on a ship called the *Caribbean Progress*, a sister ship of the *Caribbean Endeavour* trading between Miami, Puerto Barrios in Guatemala and Puerto Cortes in Honduras back to Miami. I bonded a good relationship with a Christian Mission in Barrios headed by Father Todd, a Catholic Missionary. Most of the Missionaries were American and when they went on leave and returned I gave them a free passage. We became known as *The Vatican Express*.

While on this trade schedule, my wife Jacqui joined me for a couple of months and my mum and dad moved into our house to look after the children.

On our way from Miami, we had a couple of Missionaries as passengers called Father Tom and Sister Mary who were based at El Estor in the Sierra

De Santa Cruz Mountains near Lake Izabal. They invited Jacqui to go with them to El Estor, so on our next visit to Miami Jacqui obtained a Guatemalan visa for one month. Tom and Mary had waited a week for the ship to return to Barrios and collect Jacqui for her trip to El Estor.

Jacqui's experiences were quite extraordinary. She had to travel by boat on Lake Izabal to reach El Estor. When they arrived at El Estor, they immediately departed on mule back to visit a remote Guatemalan Indian Village situated in the Sierra De Santa Cruz Mountains. The pathway up the mountainside was very narrow, with a steep drop on one side, but the mules seem to have travelled that way many times before and were sure footed.

On arrival at the village there was great excitement with everyone greeting each other as if it were for the first time and, in Jacqui's case, it was.

Jacqui front centre visiting other villages.

On one Sunday, there was a church service and a mass christening of babies attended by Indians who had walked miles from outlying villages.

Father Tom said Jacqui could attend the christenings, which were going to be held in the church, and before the christenings, he would introduce Jacqui to the natives. He told her when he indicated for her to come to the front of the church and when he introduced her she had to stand still and not be afraid because the natives as far as he knew had not seen a blonde woman before and they would come up to her and touch her all over. This was the case and they were especially interested in her legs because Jacqui was wearing tights. Several Indians came up front to inspect Jacqui; they touched her hair and ran their hands over her legs, mystified how they could be so smooth. After this inspection, Jacqui was accepted and after this occasion, they always addressed her as Madre (Mother).

Jacqui asked the Natives for permission to take photographs of the christenings, which was reluctantly given. When Jacqui had the film developed, photographs taken previously and after the christenings came out but the photographs taken at the christening did not. Very strange... Father Tom said that the natives believed that taking photographs of the babies would take their souls away.

Two weeks after leaving the ship for her missionary experience, Jacqui returned to the ship but the Immigration Officer would not let her rejoin the ship because she hadn't been in the country for a month, which was the time interval stamped in her passport. We had to get the intervention of Father Todd to persuade the Immigration Office to let Jacqui rejoin. As Father Todd employed the Immigration Officer's wife as housekeeper that must have made a difference.

We used to arrive at Puerto Barrios, Guatemala on a Wednesday night and sail on Thursday evening back to Miami. On one occasion, early one Thursday morning, I was visited by the Police informing me that two of our sailors had been caught the previous evening smoking marijuana and were in jail. I visited the two men and they sheepishly told me that they had been caught smoking "weed" in a local bar. They hadn't had any food since being put in jail and they understood that prisoners had to provide their own food. I contacted our Agent to see if we could have the men released by making a personal payment to the Chief of Police's benevolent fund but was informed that the men had been processed through the system and we could do nothing until the men stood trial, which could be in a matter of a couple of weeks. I went back to the ship and informed the crew about the situation the two sailors were in. The crew had a "whip round" and collected about a hundred dollars or so, which the bosun took to the two men so they could buy food. Then off we sailed back to Miami.

The next week in Barrios, I visited the men and they looked quite healthy and happy, chatting to the jail guards and they seemed to have the run of the jail. The crew had another "whip round" and the men were given over 100 dollars to last them the next week. The bosun told me that the men had to bribe the prison guards who organised a couple of "ladies of the night" to bring the two men cooked meals into the jail and the ladies would provide an extra service if required. No wonder the men appeared healthy and happy.

This weekly routine carried on for about five weeks with no sign of a trial on the horizon, so I instructed the crew not to give any more money to the men in jail and see what happens.

On the next visit to Barrios I found out! On the Thursday morning our agent informed me that the two men had employed a lawyer and the ship would not obtain a port clearance to sail until this incident had been cleared up. In fact, *the ship* had been arrested! The agent arranged a meeting post haste with the lawyer and we attended his offices.

On arrival at the offices, we were shown into a room, which had the unmistakable pungent smell of marijuana smoke. The lawyer and both seamen were smoking. The lawyer was quite affable, which may have been due to the effect of the marijuana, and stated he had issued a writ against the ship's owners for compensation in respect of complaints from the two seamen regarding their mistreatment by me. I pointed out that they had been arrested and jailed for smoking marijuana and by the smell in his office they were still at it. The lawyer made the observation that the charges had not been proved and when their claims for compensation were completed they would be repatriated to Trinidad without a trial.

The lawyer read statements made by the seamen stating that I had kicked them when they were doing their duties and generally ill-treated them. While the lawyer was reading the seaman's statements, they at least did have the good grace not to make eye contact and looked uncomfortable, wriggling about in their seats.

The upshot was that they were claiming six weeks salary while they had been in jail, a lump sum payment as compensation for the trauma they had endured while in prison and finally immediate repatriation to Trinidad. The lawyer had added his fees for representing the men and an additional lump sum payment for "extras", which I assumed were payments to other officials. There would be no trial and the seamen would be repatriated to Trinidad on a satisfactory conclusion of their claims.

The lawyer pointed out that the next day, Friday, was a holiday, so he would not be able to have the lien on the ship removed until the following Monday, unless an agreement was reached on the terms outlined immediately; then we could obtain a port clearance and sail that day.

The total amount to pay, about 12,000 US Dollars, was the equivalent of one day's hire for the ship. I thought paying 12,000 dollars was preferable to the ship being "off hire" for at least four days, going out of schedule and the resulting associated problems regarding informing shippers, delivery of dry and refrigerated containers at the loading berth in Miami, so I agreed to make the payment under duress. The payment would be covered by insurance in any case. The agent paid the cash on my behalf, the lien was removed, I obtained port clearance and we duly sailed Thursday night.

This voyage proved very interesting because when we were on our way back to Miami, just to the North of Cuba, we had a U.F.O. experience. It was about 10 p.m. and I was in my cabin making ready my Miami port entry papers, when I had a telephone call from the Third Mate on the bridge. He sounded very excited and asked me to come up on the navigation bridge because there was something on the starboard side he didn't understand. When I arrived on the bridge both the lookout man and the Third Mate were on the starboard side of the bridge looking at an object shaped like a disc, about 70 feet in diameter with circular lights radiating around the circumference, flying on a level with the bridge and about 100 feet away. After I had been on the bridge about two minutes the object shot off at a terrific speed and disappeared. I reported the incident to the U.S. Coast Guard, giving details regarding the shape and size of the object and the lights around the circumference, also how it had shot off with terrific speed and disappeared. They took a note of all the details and told me that several other ships had reported observing a similar phenomenon. The Coast Guard could not give any explanation for the sighting but I suppose the reports are still in the U.S.C.G. archives.

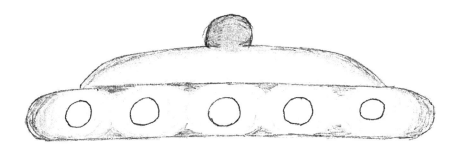

Sketch of the UFO I saw, drawn under my instructions by my son Carl Anderson. It was night but we had the Aldis signalling lamp on it. The rings round the base were lights, the rest solid.

By 1974, Common Brothers had four Roll On/Roll-Off Container Ships. The *Caribbean Progress* and the *Caribbean Endeavour* were chartered to a Miami Company called Caribbean Trailer Express and Common Brothers had opened up an office in New York and was running the *Caribbean Venture* and *Caribbean Enterprise* from New York to Kingston, Jamaica, then Boca Chica in the Dominican Republic back to New York. For a number of years I moved between these ships as Captain. I have already related some of my experiences but there are many more.

On the 18th of August 1974, I was Captain of the *Caribbean Enterprise* sailing from New York to Jamaica and the Dominican Republic. We were sailing along the Old Bahamas Channel, just North of Cuba. It was 2 a.m. and I received a telephone call from the Chief Engineer asking if it was safe to stop for a couple of hours to effect some engine repairs. I went to the navigation bridge and saw from the charts that it was safe to stop, so we stopped and just drifted along to make engine repairs. The couple of hours turned into four hours, so we got underway again at 6 a.m. Dawn was just breaking, it was cool and quiet. There was a beautiful sunrise. Sunrises and sunsets are just spectacular in this part of the world.

Due to the sea currents in that area, we had drifted north, way out of the traffic zones. Where we were the sea was dark blue and just one mile to the North of us the sea was a very pale blue, indicating the demarcation between deep water and the coral reefs, which was very pronounced. To try to gain some lost time, instead of returning to the traffic lane, I made a course skirting the coral reefs.

At 11 a.m. that day, the Third Mate telephoned me and reported that he thought there was what appeared to be a waterlogged 40-foot container floating in the water just off our port bow. I went on the navigation bridge and about five miles away there was an object in the water almost dead ahead. As we got nearer, the container turned out to be a motor yacht, half submerged, with the figure of a man standing on the deck, turned away from us. It was obvious he had not seen us approaching. I informed the engine room that we would be manoeuvring the engines immediately and the reason for doing so. I also gave the order for the motor rescue boat crew to assemble at their station. I stopped the ship about half a mile from the motor yacht and then the man seemed to sense our presence, turned around to face us, and started waving furiously. The rescue boat was lowered into the water in charge of the Chief Officer, who had a walkie-talkie for radio contact with me and off they went towards the motor yacht.

When they arrived at the yacht, the Chief Officer reported that the man was an American. The American said he was with his girlfriend but couldn't see her, which is why he was looking away from the ship and only realised we were there when he heard the engines. He was so distraught and in shock, thinking she was lost. The Chief Officer said he couldn't see anything around in the vicinity. The sea was slightly undulating and with being on the ship, which was about 80 feet distance from the waterline to the navigation bridge, I could see a fair distance. Looking through my binoculars, I spotted some flotsam (floating debris) about half a mile from the yacht. I asked the Chief Officer if he could see the flotsam but he couldn't, so I instructed him to make a circle with the rescue boat and when he was heading towards it I would let him know and then he could move in that compass direction. The exercise worked very well and off he went towards the flotsam. As he approached it, he excitedly reported that there were sharks in the area and there was a person wearing a lifejacket, floating in amongst the debris. It was the man's girlfriend, barely conscious, but the lifejacket and her face out of the water supported her head. She was lifted into the rescue boat without any delay and first aid administered. She became fully conscious during the rescue boat's return to the ship and when the boat was winched into its housing both the man and woman managed to alight from the boat with help. The whole operation from when the rescue boat was lowered into the water to being re-housed only took about 35 minutes. The couple were taken to a posh cabin designated the Owner's cabin, and given a large tot of brandy to counteract the shock. We left them to have a shower and get some rest. They had lost all their personal effects so they were given dry clothes that various crewmembers had donated. The woman was even issued with a pair of clean panties from the Third Officer's trophy collection.

The couple were Jerry Walker and Janet Vance, aged 36 and 34 respectively, both from Tennessee, U.S.A. At the time of rescue they were apparently unhurt but the next morning, after recovering from shock, it was found that Jerry had a broken finger and Janet some injury to her leg, which was a mass of bruises. I informed the U.S. Coast Guard giving them details of the rescue and asked Jerry what his insurance company was so that I could inform them of the disaster, but he told me he had not insured the boat. Jerry told me that during the night, they had hit some underwater object and at 6 a.m. that morning they thought the yacht was going down, so they had jumped into the sea. At about 10 a.m. they had seen the yacht still floating so had tried to reach the yacht again to get some more buoyant materials for themselves. Jerry had made it but Janet was then out of sight and had drifted away. To me, the rescue seemed to be Divine Intervention because we had broken down during the night and got underway again at 6 a.m. Jerry had hit an underwater object during the night and had abandoned the yacht at 6 a.m. I had decided to skirt the coral reefs and not go back into the traffic lane, which was about ten miles to the North of the ship. There was no way that Jerry and Janet would have been saved because they were so far away from the traffic lane and it was just because I decided to skirt the reefs that we came across them. I often wonder if Jerry had prayed for help.

Rescue boat approaching sinking yacht.

Jerry & Janet safely on the ship.

During our disrupted sea passage to Kingston, Jamaica, where we arrived on the 20th August, Jerry told me a personal interesting story. During the Vietnam War, he had been an aeroplane pilot on an Aircraft Carrier, which was based in the South China Sea. He had become very friendly with another pilot and after his period of service, his friend asked him what he was going to do. He said he hadn't any plans so his friend said, "Why don't you come and be my partner as a dealer in Wall Street?" Jerry said he had no experience and not the scale of funding which that career would require. "That's okay," his friend said, "I'll keep you on the right track and give you a loan to get started." That's what happened. Jerry took up the offer and on his first gamble, together with other dealers, he bought a cargo of grain that was bound for India and sold it for a vast profit before the ship carrying the grain even arrived in India. He said he seemed to have the Midas touch, kept his nose to the grindstone and before he knew it, he was a millionaire. After a couple of years he decided to take a holiday with his girlfriend. He enjoyed sailing as a hobby and always wanted to own a yacht, so he went to Fort Lauderdale in Florida, bought a motor yacht and set off towards Jamaica to visit a friend who owned a five star hotel, with the related disastrous consequences.

When we arrived in Kingston, the Immigration Authorities checked out the provided personal details of Jerry and Janet and allowed them entry into Jamaica. As they left the ship to go to their friend's hotel, Janet was very tearful and couldn't stop thanking us for saving their lives. As she left she kept saying, "I love that little ship!"

I have received a couple of letters from them since the rescue but have lost touch now. I recently wrote to them because I wanted to know if Jerry had prayed for Janet and to be saved, but they must have moved location because I didn't receive an answer.

That voyage proved eventful, because after Jerry and Janet left us and we discharged our cargo in Kingston, we loaded circus animals in the tweendecks to take to Boca Chica in the Dominican Republic, which was just a couple of days steaming distance away. We loaded a caged tiger, bear, a walk-on elephant and a bad tempered chimpanzee. During the first night's sea passage the Fourth Engineer noticed water coming into the Engine room from the tweendeck scuppers and, as Engineers do, he tasted it to see if it was fresh or salt water. It was neither—it was tiger pee. He said that put him off drinking a local beer called Tiger Beer forever and he was given the nickname Tiger, which I suppose he has to this day. When we arrived at Boca Chica, the owner of the circus was there to greet us and see how the animals had faired on their cruise. He gave me an invitation to attend the circus the next time we were in Boca Chica, which I did. I was given VIP treatment, introduced to the circus performers and audience as if I was a celebrity.

Walk on / Walk off cargo.

Spot the difference.

After we left Boca Chica, one of the seamen came to my cabin and told me that a crewmember was smuggling marijuana from Jamaica to take to New York and was stashing it in a tweendeck box beam. At 4 p.m. I went on the navigation bridge and told the Chief Officer to go and have a look in the tweendeck box beams. About ten minutes later, he came back to the bridge and told me he had looked up at one of the box beams and someone was looking down at him, so he had come for back up. We armed ourselves with heavy flashlights and went back down into the tweendeck to the box beam where the Chief Officer had seen the person looking down at him. No one was there and the Chief Officer climbed up into the box beam. After a couple of minutes he shouted, "Here it is!" and threw down ten medium sized bundles and two very large bundles of what appeared to be dried grass wrapped in brown paper. The grass was obviously marijuana, recognisable by its distinctive smell. People who use it try to disguise the smell by burning josh sticks.

I had a discussion with the Chief Officer and concluded that the person he had seen was going to relocate the marijuana to a more favourable hiding place. We decided to keep our discovery quiet and dispose of the marijuana into the sea, the reason being that if we reported the finding and kept the marijuana as evidence and the Customs authority could not discover who had been smuggling the stuff, the ship would be fined. Therefore, that's what we did.

Me & the Chief Officer, John Dagleish inspecting the contraband.

Quite a haul!

Our regular berth was pier 7 Staten Island. When we arrived we cleared customs and commenced the discharge and loading operations, which usually took 12 hours; then it was back to sea to start another voyage on our regular schedule. During the discharging operations, the person who had informed me about the marijuana smuggling came to my cabin and reported that two "heavies" had boarded the ship and were looking for the seaman who was smuggling the marijuana into the States. The seaman was hiding in the engine room in fear of his life and in fact stayed there until we sailed and were well clear of New York. It was clear that the two "heavies" had come to collect the now non-existent marijuana and would assume the seaman had done a deal for himself.

The smuggling seaman came to my cabin the next day and said he wanted to be discharged and repatriated when we arrived in Kingston, Jamaica. I told him there wasn't time to order a replacement for him this time but he could leave the following voyage. In fact, we could have sailed shorthanded but I just wanted him to sweat it out and have time to contemplate the consequences of being involved in smuggling drugs.

About three hours after we had arrived in Kingston and were well into our discharge and loading operations, I received a letter by special messenger that the Trinidadian High Commissioner wanted to see me. I duly presented myself at his opulent offices and was ushered into his presence without any delay. Our seaman was with him and the High Commissioner told him to wait in another room. Then he said to me that I had to discharge the man because he was in fear for his life. I pointed out that I would be breaking regulations by sailing under-manned but would discharge him the next time in Jamaica when I had obtained a replacement. I also pointed out that if the man was not on the ship when we sailed, he would be classed as a deserter and all expenses involved in obtaining a replacement would be deducted from his accumulated pay, which he wouldn't receive for months. I also stressed that the Trinidadian High Commission would be responsible for any costs involved for repatriation and costs while he was in their care. This statement seemed to throw a different complex on the situation. He called the man back into the room and told him that he would have to stay on the ship until the next visit to Kingston.

When we sailed from Kingston the seaman was on board and when we arrived back to New York via Boca Chica the two "heavies" again appeared and the seaman hid in the engine room from arrival to sailing. I had arranged for a replacement to join in Kingston and the smuggler was repatriated in the normal way.

I had formed a good working relationship with the work force at pier 7 Staten Island, especially the Pier Manager and his foreman Jerry who was huge and tremendously strong; I think he was the Pier Manager's minder. Whenever we were berthing or departing Jerry played the tune, 'Colonel Bogey' over the loudspeakers, greeting us and wishing us a safe voyage when we left. I suppose he thought the tune, 'Colonel Bogey' was very British!

On arrival at Staten Island, when I went to the Pier Manager's office to give him the cargo information, Jerry would pick me up and hold me over his head for a couple of minutes. This happened every time and I couldn't very well object. It caused him much amusement and I only wanted to keep on the right side of him and humour him. The Pier Manager frequently came and had lunch on the ship but one day he said, "I've been coming on your ship for lunch every time you have docked here but today I'm taking you out to lunch."

At lunchtime, he took me to this restaurant, which seemed to be very popular because it was full but the Pier Manager had reserved a table. Nearby to where we were sitting was a large circular table with eight men seated around it. The Pier Manager told me they were the local Mafia. He went on to tell me a story about the Mafia Boss coming to ask him to find some employment for his sister's son who was 28 and a bit of a bad egg. He had no option so had employed the Boss' nephew as a stevedore. One night about 11 p.m., the pier 7 security guard had phoned the Pier Manager telling him that he had found this man stealing cargo from the warehouse and asked if he should call the police. The Pier Manager said no, he would take care of things, so he telephoned the Mafia Boss and told him what had happened. The Mafia Boss told the Pier Manager to bring his nephew to a club he was at, so the Pier Manager went to pier 7 and collected the man and took him to the club. The Mafia Boss berated his nephew and slapped him across the face a couple of times, then asked the Pier Manager what he was going to do. The Pier Manager said he was going to sack him. The Mafia Boss said that he didn't want his sister on his back again and asked the Pier Manager to keep him employed; he would guarantee that his nephew wouldn't step out of line again or he would break his legs. Given this guarantee, the Pier Manager did not sack the nephew because he knew he wouldn't have any further trouble with the man.

One day while at pier 7 a man knocked on my door. He was very well dressed and I thought he was a port official. He didn't introduce himself but asked me if I would take a parcel to Kingston for him and one of the port officials would collect it. I immediately declined and didn't even ask what the parcel contained. He accepted my answer without question, didn't press me, and said, "That's okay. I just thought you might want to make some money." Then he left the ship. I told the Pier Manager about the incident and he remarked that the parcel was probably a bundle of cash in payment for drugs and it was a good job I didn't accept and get myself involved. Later, thinking about the incident, I am sure the Pier Manager was involved and had recommended me as a trustworthy courier, because how would he have known what the parcel contained? It appeared more than an assumption on his part.

At the end of 1974, the time charter of the *Caribbean Endeavour* and *Progress* to the Miami Company had come to an end and the two vessels were engaged on alternative charters. I was Captain of the *Endeavour* and we had been time chartered to a company called Canadian Pacific, to load trailers and automobiles in St. John, New Brunswick, Canada and discharge in St. John's, Newfoundland.

After loading in St. John, New Brunswick, and on our way to St. John's, Newfoundland, the Chief Engineer, Peter Hughes and I were having a pre-lunch drink in my cabin and he made the observation that I would look much younger if I had my hair dyed. Although I had a good crop of curly hair, it had become completely grey when I was only 32. He said that he dyed his hair and he would do mine with his dye which would result in a rich brown colour. I agreed, and Peter got his dye and set to work on one side of my head. After a while, he couldn't contain himself and went into fits of laughter. When I asked him what he was laughing at he said that he had run out of dye with only one side of my head treated. I looked in the mirror and discovered I was piebald, one side of my hair grey and the other side brown. I suppose it would have been in style today, but not then.

As we steamed along a Northerly course on the east side of Newfoundland towards St. John's, an easterly wind was causing the pack ice to drift in towards the land. We had to hug the coast and when we managed to get into St. John's at 6 p.m., the pack ice was only one mile away. The next morning the harbour was completely filled with thick ice. After discharging, I went up "Lookout Hill", a high point from where you could clearly see the extent of the pack ice intermingled with large icebergs. I was resigned to being bottled up in St. John's until the wind changed to a Westerly direction. We were stuck in St. John's for eight days but it gave me plenty of time to buy a large bottle of dye to complete my hairdo.

It was decided to change our discharge port in Newfoundland to a port called Argentia, which was in a more sheltered area and relatively ice-free. The *Endeavour* was the largest ship ever to dock in Argentia and it seemed as if the whole town had come to greet us when we docked.

During the period of trading to Argentia, we formed a good working relationship with the Custom Officer and a sergeant of the Canadian Mounted Police and I invited them and their wives to an evening meal and social evening of drinks and a game of darts in the ship's bar, which became a weekly event our friends looked forward to, as did we.

Receiving a pewter tankard from the Royal Canadian Mounted Police
Sergeant, Chief of Customs pictured to the right.

After a couple of voyages, there were complaints that the trailers were being broached and cargo stolen, mainly cases of whisky. I made astute enquiries and discovered that one of the able seamen was the culprit and was selling his ill-gotten gains to some servicemen from the nearby American Air force Base. I arranged with the Mounted Police Sergeant to conduct a search of the crew's accommodation and had instant success. The suspected able seaman's cabin was like a pub storeroom of whisky. I don't know where he could have slept because his bunk was also full of cases of whisky. I had the Sergeant take the man into custody. About an hour later, the Sergeant came to the ship and told me that the local judge wanted to see me because the seaman was going to be processed immediately before the ship sailed.

I accompanied the Sergeant to meet the judge, who was a very nice person and greeted me like a friend.

"Captain!" he said, "What are we going to do with this man? The longest sentence in jail is six months, or we can fine him in lieu. I don't want to give him a prison sentence because the expense of keeping him in jail falls on our government. If we fine him, what do you think he will be able to afford?"

"Well," I suggested, "he gets $300 a month wages and he has that in the ship so maybe you could fine him that amount and then we will send him back to Trinidad."

"That seems the perfect solution!" the judge exclaimed. "We'll hold the court hearing now before you sail."

There was the judge, the clerk of the court and myself attending in the court. The Sergeant brought the seaman into the court from the jail and placed him on the stand.

The Judge read out the charge of the pilfering of cargo. The seaman pleaded guilty.

Then the judge explained that he could sentence him to six months in prison, but that I had spoken up for the man so he was only going to fine him $300 and he would be sent back to Trinidad on the first available flight.

The seaman reached into his pocket and brought out a roll of notes that would have choked a horse and started counting off $300 and tried to give it to the Judge.

"No, give that to the Clerk of the Court!" the Judge exclaimed, and added, "And you can thank Captain Anderson that it isn't a six month jail sentence."

The hearing was concluded to the satisfaction of all concerned, including the seaman who had escaped a prison sentence, and our Agent made arrangements for him to be repatriated to Trinidad after we had sailed from Agentia.

After completing our time charter to Canadian Pacific in 1976 we were chartered by a company called Utterwick on time charter, scheduled to load in Genoa, Italy, and discharge in Jeddah, Saudi Arabia.

Leaving Genoa, we sailed southerly, passing through the Messina Straits between Italy and Sicily, then made an Easterly course to Port Said, Egypt. After transiting the Suez Canal, we made a southerly course to arrive at Jeddah in the Red Sea.

When we arrived at Jeddah, there were several ships at anchor awaiting docking pilots. The ships were boarded by pilots and docked in order of arrival.

The pilot boarded to dock us and when we tried to heave up the anchor, the windlass would not work and the Chief Engineer told me it would take about an hour to repair. The pilot asked me what was wrong and I told him we were having a little trouble with the windlass but it wouldn't take long to fix. He informed me that he would wait for ten minutes, then he would have to leave and we would revert to the back of the list in order of docking.

I engaged him in conversation in the hope of hitting onto a subject he was interested in so that he wouldn't notice the length of time it was taking to repair the windlass. He didn't seem interested in anything until I mentioned football—then I couldn't stop him talking. Apparently, he was a member of a new team called the North Star Football Club and they were having difficulty getting football gear and strips.

I told him I would get him the gear and strip from Genoa because we were going to be on a regular run from Genoa to Jeddah for the next three months. He said he had asked other Captains to bring him things from abroad but they never did. I assured him I would, even drew the outline of a shirt, and suggested that as the club was named the North Star Football Team, the figure of a star would look good on the pocket. As a joke, I put the Star of David on the pocket, which he didn't pick up. He got quite excited and by the time we had finished talking about the amount of gear and strips he needed, the windlass had been repaired, so we heaved up the anchor and docked in our berth.

The pilot left the ship to go directly to a meeting of his team, all excited, with the drawing of the shirt.

Thirty minutes later he came running back to the ship saying, "No no no, not this star!" I explained it was my warped sense of humour and I wouldn't order the shirts with the Israelis Star of David but a star with five points.

When we arrived back in Genoa to load, I ordered the football gear and strip from a sports shop, to be collected the next visit.

Approaching Jeddah for the second visit there were three ships ahead of me for pilots, but the pilot boat bypassed them and my foot-balling friend boarded me, much to the consternation of the Captains of the ships bypassed. The pilot asked me where the football gear was and when I told him I had ordered it and would pick it up the next time in Genoa, he was crestfallen and acted as if he didn't believe me.

I collected the football gear and strip the next time in Genoa and obtained a receipt for the goods. Arriving back in Jeddah, the pilot boat again bypassed the ships ahead of me and came directly to us. Our foot-balling pilot friend could hardly contain himself when I told him I had the gear. He wasn't interested in piloting; he first wanted to see the shirts, shorts and socks! After the first flush of excitement, I gave him the receipt and he said, "I must tell you Captain, you are the first Captain who has given me a receipt for anything I asked them to bring in for me!"

He tried to give me $200 extra for bringing the gear in but I told him I didn't want any reward and was only too pleased to be of help.

I never had to wait for a pilot at Jeddah. We always had VIP treatment and I suppose the North Star Football Team is still operating.

In November 1977, I was Captain on the *Caribbean Progress* and we had been fixed on a voyage charter to the Hoegh Line, loading in Rotterdam for discharge in Lagos, Nigeria.

On arrival Rotterdam to load, the ship's agent boarded and after discussing the cargo to be loaded, which was prefabricated sections of airport passenger walkways on trailers, he informed me that piracy was rife off Lagos, relating that pirates had recently boarded a small Danish vessel and had violently robbed the crew members, killing one of them. Now, most ships at anchor, awaiting a berth, at night, lifted up their anchor, proceeded about ten miles off shore, and drifted until daylight, coming back inshore to anchor during daylight hours.

He then asked me what kind of weapon I would like just in case pirates boarded us. He gave me a choice of shotguns, machine guns or handguns. I told him I didn't want any but he insisted that for our own safety I should choose something, so I chose a double-barrelled shotgun.

After leaving Rotterdam and arriving at Lagos, we had to anchor and await a berth. There were about 30 ships anchored and at night, we all weighed anchor, steamed about ten miles from the coast, and drifted until daylight. That is, all except a couple of Russian Ships that remained at anchor.

Fortunately, we had a priority cargo and would only take about eight hours to discharge, so were only a couple of days delayed. Some ships had been at anchor for months.

When the pilot boarded to take us to our berth, I asked him why the Russian ships didn't weigh anchor at night and drift ten miles off the coast. He told me that they had armed security guards on board and the pirates didn't meddle with the Russians, especially since the pirates had boarded a Russian freezer ship, had been rounded up by the armed security guards and put in a deep freezer for the night. The next morning the pirates were as stiff as boards and they had been thrown overboard. The story had got around and the pirates didn't bother Russian ships.

After discharging in Lagos without any problems, I received orders to sail back to Rotterdam.

On the 17th November at ll:45 a.m. in a position about 200 miles South West of the Canary Islands, a fuel pipe on the starboard engine fractured, spraying hot oil onto the port engine exhaust, which caused an immediate raging inferno. The engine room was evacuated of personnel and procedures put in place to contain and hopefully eventually extinguish the fire.

When I had been promoted to Captain, whichever ship I commanded, I had initiated specific fire-fighting procedures at fire drills, especially in the areas where fires would be likely to start, e.g. engine room, galley, accommodation, etc.

If a fire occurred in the engine room, each crewmember was assigned a specific duty, closing all ventilators, shutting off the oil supply from a control panel on the open deck to the engines, generators and the forced draught fans. A muster roll would be taken to make sure everyone was accounted for. Then a permanently fixed piped fire fighting system of carbon dioxide, which was stored in bottles, was introduced into the engine room, the idea being that if all the ventilators had been closed to exclude air, the carbon dioxide would act like a gas blanket over the fire so that the fire would be extinguished through lack of air.

The specialized fire drills proved successful and eventually, by 5 p.m. the fire seemed to have been extinguished, but after consulting the Chief Engineer, Adrian Chapman, we decided to keep the engine room closed until the following morning to ensure the fire had been completely extinguished, so that when we opened up, the inrush of air would not re-ignite the fire, as we had already used up the supply of carbon dioxide.

There was no electricity, so the engineers fashioned a barbecue from empty steel drums and the crew gathered on the open deck for a barbecue of baked beans, potatoes, sausages and steaks. After the barbecue, all the crew gathered in the Officer's candlelit bar where we had drinks and horse racing games. It was quite an occasion and lifted the crew's spirits.

In the meantime, thanks to a battery back-up system for the radio communications, I had informed the Company about the fire and what I intended to do. A salvage tug owned by a company called Smitt, stationed in the Canary Islands, must have picked up my telephone conversation with Common Brothers because they have a 24-hour listening watch on the radio.

At 6 a.m. the next morning a Smitt Salvage Tug appeared and stated that he had been ordered by our Owners to tow us into Las Palmas in the Canary Isles for repairs. I told him to wait until we had investigated the engine room.

We opened up the engine room to assess the damage. The port engine was a mess and unfortunately the cabling for the electrical power supply to the navigation bridge ran above the port engine and the cabling was just a melted mass, so we had no navigational systems or steering. The starboard engine and generators appeared okay.

Adrian, the Chief Engineer, made several tests and said we could get underway on the starboard engine only and although the power supply to the navigation bridge had been knocked out we could lead cabling from the engine room generators to the emergency steering compartment on the poop deck.

I informed Common Brothers of the current state of the ship and what we intended to do and also that I was positive we would be able to proceed under our own power to Las Palmas, so we would not require the assistance of the salvage tug.

Every crewmember, even the cook and stewards, assisted in running cabling from the engine room to the emergency steering compartment. The engineers had their work cut out disconnecting the melted cabling and connecting the temporary cabling.

At 2 p.m. we were ready to test the starboard engine and emergency steering gear. On the bridge, I was in contact by walkie-talkie radio to the seaman who was controlling the steering on the poop deck. It worked. Then we started the starboard engine and proceeded on our way.

I informed Common Brothers of the good news and rejected the salvage tug's towing services, although he remained with us until 6 p.m. in case we broke down.

On arrival at Las Palmas, Foster Davison, our Senior Superintendent, joined us to co-ordinate temporary repairs to the port engine and re-run of cabling to the navigation bridge, which took 14 days before we could continue our voyage to the U.K. In fact, we dry-docked in Newcastle-upon-Tyne for permanent repairs.

While we were in Las Palmas, Veronica, Adrian Chapman's wife, joined the ship. One night our Agent invited Foster Davison, myself, Adrian and Veronica to a rather "posh" restaurant. Veronica has a very outgoing personality and is up for anything. I surreptitiously approached the restaurant manager and asked him if he recognised the lady at the table. I told him Veronica was a very well known singer in England and if he asked her nicely she might sing a couple of songs and give his customers a moment of magic they would never forget. He did ask Veronica to sing and although she was surprised at this request, Veronica, being Veronica, readily agreed. The restaurant pianist, sitting at a grand piano, asked her what key she wanted to sing in and she replied, "Any." After a suitable introduction by the manager, which again surprised Veronica, she went into her song, got carried away and added a high kicking dance routine. The customers must have thought it was a comedy act but they enjoyed it judging by the enthusiastic applause at the completion of the performance. The manager thanked her but didn't ask her to give an encore. I had to admit later to Veronica that I was the instigator of the ruse.

While in Newcastle, a representative from the underwriters (insurance company) for the ship visited the *Progress* and presented all the crewmembers with silver tankards. Adrian and I received a silver plate commemorating the incident. I recently donated my silver plate to the Hull Trinity House Corporation silver collection, which can be viewed by visitors during their tour of the "House".

Silver plate presented by Underwriters.

In July 1978, I was Captain of a ship called the *Aspen Trader*, a vessel that Common Brothers operated and managed for another Company. The Deck Officers and Engineers were British and the rest of the crew Philipinoes.

We had loaded a general cargo at Manila in the Philippines for discharge at Nampo in North Korea. On completing discharge in Nampo we sailed to Chungjin to load a part cargo of steel plates.

When we arrived at Chungjin and docked, the ship's agent told us that he had arranged for us to visit a local girls' school whose ages ranged from 11 to 15. Six of the ship's officers accompanied me.

A bus had been arranged to transport us from the ship to the school. The road was quite wide and appeared new but there was hardly any motorized traffic on it, just a few people cycling. I noticed, as we passed some high-rise flats, that the windows didn't have any curtains. I asked our guide why the windows didn't have curtains and he stated that it was a waste of materials and no one had curtains.

It was raining when we arrived at the school and some of the older girls were waiting with umbrellas to escort us from the bus into the school. All the girls were in identical uniforms, blue gym slips with white blouses, and all said in unison, "Welcome to our school."

The Headmistress then showed us around.

As we entered the first classroom, the girls all clapped and to our surprise, they were learning to send and receive Morse code. A girl at the teacher's deck sent us a welcome message in English. As we left the classroom, the girls all clapped again.

Then we had a quick look around the biology room, a room containing all kinds of stuffed Korean animals and birds and jars of pickled animal parts.

Biology room.

Next, we were shown a Young Pioneers class, made up of girls who had achieved good marks in all subjects. They seemed to be engaged in a general discussion, no doubt political.

Then on to the Political Education room where they studied the early revolutionary activities of The Great Leader, Comrade Kim IL Sung, and the history of the Liberation from the Japanese Imperialist aggressors. A large bust of The Great Leader occupied the front of the classroom.

We were then taken on to the "gym", which was a long room, empty except for a group of girls who ran towards us, grabbed our arms and took us to the place we had to stand and watch their display of athletics and ballet, for which we were proudly informed by the Headmistress they had won several medals including a gold medal for their ballet performance at one of their National events. Our interpreter informed us that many of the girls would become professionals on completion of their schooling.

Dance group & ship's officers.

First, they demonstrated quite a professional standard of tumbling and exercises, and then the girls singing, dancing, and playing musical instruments and a series of ballet dances entertained us. They did not show any signs of shyness or embarrassment and in fact seemed to enjoy performing for us.

One dance depicted the dejection of two students who had only managed good marks in two out of the three necessary areas of learning, namely art, sport and academic subjects. They were miserable because they hadn't achieved the standard required to become Young Pioneers, but as their weak subjects were different, they helped each other, finally achieving the necessary standard in the three areas of learning and were welcomed by the group as Young Pioneers with much excitement and happiness.

It was noticeable how well they expressed their role feelings by the use of their heads, eyes and facial expressions with raised eyebrows, wide eyes, beaming smile, lips pursed and the shrugging of shoulders.

The next dance routine came as a bit of a shock to us. We were told that this dance routine was a call to oppressed students of Asia, Africa and Latin America to rise up and overthrow the U.S. imperialistic aggressors. About ten girls entered the room in pairs dressed in the various fashions of these continents, each carrying a wooden rifle.

One girl carried a wooden life-size figure of an American soldier with detachable parts into the room. The girls with the wooden guns lined up in front of the effigy of the American soldier and pointed their guns at him. The teacher banged a drum and the detachable head fell off. The arms and legs followed in time with the drum and then the corpse was dragged out of the room amid enthusiastic clapping.

After the completion of the dance routines, we were again grabbed and marched outside with the girls all singing. I presented a stereo radio/tape recorder to the Headmistress as a memento of our visit, which, after a nervous look at our interpreter, who gave a hardly noticeable nod, she accepted.

Suitable departing speeches were made; we were yet again mobbed by the girls and escorted in song to the bus.

The bus took us to a large hotel, which seemed quite empty except for our party. In the reception area of the hotel there were numerous display cabinets full of hand crafted Korean merchandise marked up in sterling; they also accepted "U.S. imperialist dollars", so we assumed it was a "tourist" hotel. I bought some lovely silk embroidered scenes of North Korea.

After the interval for shopping, the hotel manager and several waiters escorted us to the dining room for lunch. We were the only occupants of the room and were quickly served a delicious soup, followed by a main course of whole crab, prawns and chicken with a side salad and ice cream desert. All washed down with a few bottles of imperialist Japanese beer.

On our way back to the ship, the bus stopped at an enormous bronze statue of the Great Leader to have our photographs taken, for the Koreans records I suppose.

While in Chungjin a football match was arranged, which was supposed to be between the ship and the Agents. When I had arranged the match with the Agent, he had asked me if we were very good and I laid it on a bit thick how very, very good we were. He looked a bit worried.

We were taken by bus to the football ground and were surprised to see hundreds of spectators, mainly children, standing along the sidelines of the pitch. The Agent's team was already stripped for action so we got changed into our football strip and ran onto the pitch in single file like the professionals do, to loud applause. The match ended 9-nil to the Agents. Every time they scored, the Koreans went wild. When the match finished we were surprised to see nine of the Agent's team struggling back into their army uniforms and boarding an army truck for their departure.

We concluded that I had scared the Agent with my outrageous boasting about our prowess at football and he did not want to lose face if they lost the match, so he had commandeered the services of the army football team.

On completion of part loading in Chungjin, we sailed towards Heungnam to complete loading.

We arrived on the 24th of July 1978 and were ordered to anchor and await further instructions. Two port officials boarded the ship and told me that we would have to remain at anchor until after the 27th of July, which was the 25th Anniversary of the end of the Korean War. They also informed me that there was going to be a Captain's meeting that night; all the Captains of the ships in port would be attending, and I would have to chair the meeting because I was English and if I did not attend, the ship may remain at anchor for some considerable time.

I duly attended the meeting and the room began to fill with all the sea captains, about 12, and a group of North Koreans. The sea captains were mainly captains from Communist countries, Russia, China, Poland and North Korea, except for one other captain who was from India. I told the Indian Captain that the North Koreans had appointed me to chair the meeting or my ship would be delayed. He related that he had received similar threats about attending the meeting.

When the meeting started, the Indian captain sat next to me. A North Korean representative, who seemed to be in charge, began proceedings by informing the gathering that I would be chairing the meeting. I immediately stood up and announced that it was not democratic for them to appoint a chairman; it should be the captains who should choose a chairman and I recommended the Polish captain. I gave a nudge to the Indian captain who immediately seconded my proposal. The North Koreans went in a huddle and the Polish captain came over to me and told me that he couldn't chair the meeting. He said it was more than his job was worth to rock the boat, so to speak.

The North Korean huddle separated and the man in charge said that the Polish captain was going to propose me as chairman, which was seconded by a Russian captain and the proposal was overwhelmingly accepted.

The agenda for the meeting had been prepared for me and only consisted of one item—that each ship had to provide ten crewmembers to attend a celebratory meeting on the 27th of July in the great hall to commemorate the great victory attained by the Korean people against the U.S. imperialists.

The meeting was followed by us all being escorted to a darkened hall where a propaganda film was shown. It was about "the awful conditions being experienced by the people in South Korea." One scene, I remember, was a below the waist view of someone dressed in a U.S. soldier's immaculate uniform and highly polished boots, standing in all this sand and a small child reaching up with an empty bowl as if begging some food and the soldier swiping the child across the face. Each of us had a Korean sitting behind us like a voice of conscience, explaining that people in South Korean were starving and this is how the American imperialists treated them. At the time, I thought in making the film, how could the director have shown the soldier from the waist down, in an immaculate uniform and highly polished boots without a speck of sand on them, with all the sand around.

The next morning I had another visit from the two port officials who presented me with a letter supposedly written by me, which, as chairman, I had to read at the meeting on the 27th July. I still have the copy and it read like this:

HIS EXCELLENCY KIM IL SUNG
PRESIDENT OF THE DEMOCRATIC PEOPLE'S REPUBLIC OF KOREA

Your Excellency Great President

On the 25th Anniversary of the victory of the Korean People's Fatherland Liberation War, we held a meeting to celebrate with the crew of many countries and have the greatest honour to bring this congratulatory letter to Your Excellency Great President.

The great victory attained by the heroic Korean people under the seasoned leadership of Your Excellency most outstanding and Great President is the great event of mankind that brought about the starting of decline for the U.S. imperialists who boasted of being the "strongest" in the world for the first time in their history.

Only leading the most severe national liberation war to victory Your Excellency Great President in the van of the struggle against U.S. Imperialists created the brilliant model and made small county Korea might and great.

The U.S. Imperialists up to now 25 years has passed since they were defeated in Korea, do not give up the design to invade Korea and resort further to a new war provocative manoeuvrings while instigating PAK JUNG HI puppet clique in South Korea.

They are manoeuvring to permanently split Korea into two in an attempt to turn Korea into a dangerous war field of Far East, ignoring the resolution of the 30th U.N.G.A. and introducing nuclear weapons.

We cannot recognise the "Two Koreas" policy of the USA authorities and condemn it sternly. We will render our full support and solidarity to the

Korean people's struggle for withdrawing all foreign forces out of South Korea and for the independent and peaceful reunification of the country.

USA authorities should cease the war provocative manoeuvrings in South Korea and withdraw all armed forces at once considering significantly the voices of the political parties and social organisations in Asia, Africa and Europe who are desiring the Koreas Reunification.

Victory belongs to the Korean People fighting for justice.

We reverently wish a long life in the best health to your Excellency Great President for the independent and peaceful reunification of Korea and for the boundless prosperity of your country.

After reading the letter, I told them that I couldn't read that at the meeting. It wasn't the type of phrases I would use but I would compose a letter of my own which they could view the next day. After some discussion amongst themselves, they agreed with my suggestion, accompanied with a veiled threat that the ship would not be loaded if the letter were not read out at the meeting.

This was the letter I composed:

This is a momentous occasion and a great honour for me as chairman of the sea captains in Heungnam to be allowed to send greetings to President KIM IL SUNG on the 25th Anniversary of the foundation of the Democratic People's Republic of Korea.

To show seafarers solidarity with the people of the D.P.R. of Korea, in their aspirations of reunification, I am suggesting that seafarers all over the world should spread the word, the word being PAXO. Pax being Latin for peace and O for organisation. I want the Captains and Crewmembers in this hall to carry the message, start their own PAXO groups, and show that the PAXO group is not a trifle thing. [PAXO is the brand name for seasoned stuffing.]

Let our PAXO group be like a small pebble being thrown into a pond and the resulting ripples radiating to the edge of the pond as I hope the initiation of our PAXO group will radiate to the ends of the earth.

To conclude, to show our solidarity with the D.P.R. of Korea, when I shout the D.P.R. of Korea, I want you to reply PAXO.

Gentlemen, in moving a vote of thanks to the Captains and Crewmembers of the ships in this port and also to the Assistant Port Director for the loan of this hall, I wish to thank you in showing your support to your Captains in this meeting, also that as seafarers we are not politically minded so hope you take the contents of this meeting in the context they are meant.

The next day, the two port officials boarded the ship, read the letter I had prepared and were quite impressed, especially with the PAXO theme and the pebble in the pond idea, but they insisted that I had to read their letter out or we would be delayed loading. I thought, well, people in higher places would know that the phraseology is not what I would have chosen. The alternative to reading their letter out was being delayed for some considerable time in Heungnam, so I thought reading their letter was the lesser of the two evils, so agreed to read their letter out at the meeting.

We were brought to our berth on the 26th all ready to commence loading on the 28th. On the morning of the 27th, the 25th Anniversary of the end of the Korean War, the Second Engineer and I were escorted to a statue of Kim IL Sung and were presented with a basket of flowers to lie in front of the statue.

In the evening, I arrived at the meeting hall with ten of my crewmembers. The hall was packed out to overflowing. When the meeting started, the Captain of each ship went up in turn on stage and read his letter, which had been prepared by the North Koreans. I was the last to speak and when I stood on the podium facing the gathering, I was greeted by the sight of about ten Filipinos seated in the front row with huge grins on their faces, all wearing identical "T" shirts with the wording, "God Bless America" in bold lettering on the front. I gave them a wink and nod, then went into my spiel, which had been prepared for me but added the last paragraph I had written as an alternative speech.

Reluctantly giving my speech.

The meeting broke up and we all returned to our ships to find out that loading had already commenced.

The next day some Korean Officials came with transport to take a group of us for a tour of the capital P'yongyang. One of the attractions was to visit the underground transport service. As we went from ground level to the rail platform, I thought to myself that the area down to the platform could readily be converted to a missile launching pad. A train pulled into the station and as if by luck when it stopped, an empty carriage faced us. It was immaculate and had obviously just been cleaned and made pristine for our benefit. A guard was stationed to stop any Korean passengers boarding that particular carriage. We had a pleasant tour of P'yongyang and everywhere we went we were the centre of attraction. Everywhere was very clean and well maintained, although there was no vehicular traffic evident.

We completed loading five days later and sailed off into the wide blue yonder with grateful thanks that our time in North Korea had ended and no major incidents had occurred.

While in North Korea we had been continually photographed, for propaganda purposes I suppose, and I wouldn't be surprised to learn that we had been filmed at the Captains' Meeting, but I'm sure the front row of Filipino seamen wouldn't have been shown.

Chapter Six

Passenger Ship Captain Years

S.S. Veracruz

IN 1981 COMMON BROTHERS bought a Passenger Vessel named *Veracruz*, which was owned by the Bahama Cruise Line. The story circulating at the time about how the Company came to acquire the *Veracruz* is interesting, and I have no reason to doubt the story, knowing the people involved. Apparently, John and Sandy Common were at a Ship Owner's meeting being held in London, where they met Mr del Valle, who was the President of the Bahama Cruise Line, a company based in Miami, Florida. That Company had financial problems and Mr del Valle, who was a very personable, persuasive salesman, convinced Mr John and Sandy that Cruising was a very lucrative business.

The upshot was that Mr Foster Davison, Chief Superintendent for Common Brothers and I were sent to inspect the ship in a cruise-working environment. At that time, the ship was cruising in the West Indies, sailing from Puerto Rico to Saint Thomas, Antigua, Guadeloupe and Barbados back to Puerto Rico, a two-week round trip cruise.

Mr. Davison and I joined the vessel in Puerto Rico and were given V.I.P. treatment from Mr del Valle and the German Captain, Captain Thorne. We were accommodated in the best cabins and received preferential treatment from the crew, also free bar facilities. I imagine the crew had been instructed to give us every co-operation and only give positive glowing reports to our inquiries, which they did. I suppose they were all hoping to keep their jobs.

Considering her age, the *Veracruz* was in good structural condition, although the main boilers and sewage system needed urgent attention. The crew, under

95

the guidance of Captain Thorne, kept the ship immaculate including cabins, public areas, dining rooms and outside deck and hull paintwork.

On completion of the two-week cruise, Mr Davison and I went back to the offices in Newcastle to give our written reports and so the *Veracruz* was purchased.

The history of the *Veracruz* is very interesting. She was built in 1957 by Deutsche Werft, Hamburg, as the *Theodor Herzl*, founder of the Zionist movement, part of a reparations pact between West Germany and Israel for the German Second World War atrocities against the Jewish people. The ship was initially operated by Zim Line in the Mediterranean. In 1964, she was converted to a one-class cruise ship and sold in 1969 to the American International Service Travel Services and renamed the *Carnivale*, operating in the Caribbean as a floating luxury hotel. In 1975 she was sold to the New Horizons Shipping Limited, re-built to accommodate about 800 passengers and about 280 crew, renamed *Freeport* and employed on the Miami/Nassau/Freeport/Miami cruise run. That is when Mr del Valle and Captain Thorne became involved. In 1976 she was renamed *Veracruz* and employed mainly in the West Indies. Then in 1981 Common Brothers became involved.

The *Veracruz* was registered in Panama, to avoid taxes, crew salary and manning restrictions. There were about 12 different nationalities of crewmembers including German, British, Greek, French, American, South Korean, Indonesian, Honduranian, Jamaican, Canadian, Filipino and Lebanese.

The captain, Captain Thorne, I suppose, was everyone's idea, especially the ladies, of what a passenger ship captain should look like. He was a bachelor, about 35-years-old, quite good looking with gleaming white capped teeth, a good physique and very fit. He had converted the adjacent cabin to his into an exercise room and fitted with work-out equipment. He was very strict with the crew, popular with passengers but not so much with the crew. He was gifted with an outstanding ability of ship handling in docking/undocking or emergency situations; in fact, I have not encountered a more proficient ship-handling master.

The Chief Purser, George Reilly, was an American and in charge of preparing port entry/exit papers, engaging/discharging crew members and calculating crew wages, overseeing embarkation/disembarkation of passenger procedures, collecting and auditing the cash results of all bar, tour and casino transactions. He was the ideal Chief Purser, and his good looks, personality and unflappable demeanour was a definite asset to the ship.

The two berth cabins on the *Veracruz* were very small and at embarkation time, passengers complaining about the size of their allotted cabins and demanding changes invaded the reception area. George would give them a very generous bar chit and assure the complainants he would do his best to accommodate them. By the time the ship sailed most of the complainants were in a happy mood and told George not to bother changing their cabins; after all, they would only be sleeping in them and using the washing facilities. George's generous bar chit ploy seemed to work every time—well, almost. He had as staff, one Assistant Purser and four Purserettes who were all female, a mixture of English, American, Canadian and one Lebanese girl, Renee. The Purserettes doubled as tour guides, assisting in passenger daytime activities and spotlight operators for the evening shows.

The Hotel Manager, Jon Pierre, was French, had an engaging manner and the ability of quick repartee when he occasionally gave cookery lessons to the passengers as an extra activity on the cruise. He was in charge of planning the menus, ordering all the food requirements for the voyage and in charge of all the cooks, waiters and other catering staff including cleaning staff. Most of the catering staff was Jamaican but the midnight snack ice figure carvings were created by artistic Filipino waiters. In today's climate of incessant TV cookery shows, Jon Pierre, if he had wanted, could also have had a very successful career as a TV Chef.

The Chief Steward, Mr Ham, was South Korean, very muscular and hard as nails. He had been in the South Korean Army Special Forces during the Korean War. Mr Ham was in charge of the cabin stewards and laundry staff, who were mainly South Korean with a smattering of Indonesian and Haitian personnel. None of his staff ever stepped out of line. The cabins, alleyways and public areas were always immaculate. Mr Ham also doubled as a "minder" and head of security. I had reason to be thankful for his services on one occasion while on a "Cruise to Nowhere" which I will relate later in this book.

The bar manager Mr Choe was South Korean, as were the bartenders and waiters. He was responsible to the Hotel Manager for the efficient working of the Bar Department.

The resident Entertainment Staff were headed by the Cruise Director, Cliff Nelson, an English Comedian/Singer, who had permanently relocated to Florida. By modern day standards of TV entertainers, Cliff could have had a successful TV career in England. He was responsible for arranging the entertainment, tours and shipboard activities for passengers during the cruise. The Entertainment Staff consisted of an Assistant Cruise Director, Paul Lombardino, who had an incredible singing voice and had an evening show of his own—an American Big Band Sound, a Filipino band called "The Manila Connection" and a Filipino trio who played in the bar adjacent to the casino. All these resident acts were superb. There were also various additional acts that were engaged on a voyage-to-voyage basis. Most of the Filipino entertainers met and married staff and passengers during the time they were on the ship and eventually settled in the States. In fact, the drummer of the Manila Connection married our Passenger Liaison Manager, Shirley Peak.

The engine room staff were a mixture of Filipino Officers and Honduranian crew with Filipino Air Conditioning Officers and South Korean Electrical Officers.

The deck crew were Honduran.

The Doctor, Willie Abadan and his wife, who was the nurse but also a qualified doctor, were both Filipino. The Casino personnel were also Filipino.

When Common Brothers took over the Bahama Cruise Line they retained Mr del Valle as President and Captain Thorne as Master of the *Veracruz*. To have a Common Brother's presence, I was appointed Staff Captain and my remit was to learn the intricacies of running a cruise ship and the difference between loading general cargoes and the loading and care of passengers during their cruise experience. David Lynn, a real dyed in the wool Common Brother's employee, was appointed Chief Engineer.

Soon after joining, before David came, the *Veracruz* had main boiler problems and we were stuck in Antigua where a specialist from Babcock and Wilcox, the boilermakers, had been despatched to advise us on repairs. Mr Davison, Chief Superintendent, had also been sent to co-ordinate repairs. The passengers had no hot water for bathing and were in an ugly mood. The Greek Chief Engineer had taken to his bed, with all the worry I suppose. I didn't wear my white uniform but a boiler suit as a disguise, also using the working alleyway to avoid irate passengers.

When the specialist arrived, I met him at the gangway in my boiler suit disguise. He wanted to get started straight away with his inspection so I took him to the engineers' changing room, where he changed into his boiler suit. When we left the changing room we came to a door and he asked me if we could get to the engine room via that door. I said I didn't know, I had only been on the ship one week. He gave me a strange look of disbelief, opened the door, which led into the engine room. He went down to the boiler room with me in tow, asking technical questions to which I had no answers and his incredulous looks seemed to become permanent. On reaching the boiler room, I introduced him to Mr Davison and the three of us went inside the boiler to view the damage. After the boiler inspection, which took about one hour, I suggested we went for lunch because by that time it was about 1 p.m.

We arrived at the Officer's dinning room, ordered lunch and Mr Davison engaged the specialist in discussions regarding what would be required and the length of time the repairs would take. In the course of these discussions, Mr Davison addressed me as Captain. The specialist exclaimed, "Are *you* the Captain?" "Well, Staff Captain," I replied. He breathed a sigh of relief and said in a relieved manner, "Oh, thank God for that, I thought you were the Chief Engineer!" It was then I realised I had not introduced myself when I met him at the gangway and understood the resulting incredulous looks regarding my answers to his queries was because he thought I was the Chief Engineer.

The boiler repairs proved to be a very expensive exercise because passengers had to be repatriated and one cruise cancelled.

Very soon after the boiler problems, the itinerary was changed from the West Indies Islands, making Tampa, Florida, the home port and sailing to Mexico back to Tampa.

I continued my learning curve at Tampa, the embarkation port, by observing the procedure checking in passengers for boarding. The passengers' tickets were checked and they were issued with a boarding pass, luggage sent to an assembly area, transported to the ship and delivered by the cabin stewards to the appropriate cabins. The passengers then went to a point that had been set up by the Maitre d'Hotel to request first or second sitting for meals and be assigned their dining table number. As they went up the gangway onto the ship, the ship's photographers took their photographs as a memento to be bought later in the cruise.

Regarding dining room seating arrangements, Captain Thorne always took the evening meal second seating at 8 p.m. and had a table that accommodated ten passengers. The company provided the captain with a list of V.I.P.'s and for them to have a captain's table invite sometime during the cruise. Repeat passengers always received V.I.P. treatment and an invite to the Captain's Table. One couple enjoyed the experience on the *Veracruz* so much, they made 26 repeat cruises spanning the time before I joined the ship in 1981 up to the time I left the ship in 1985.

Additional guests to the captain's table were the captain's own choice and any remaining vacancies chosen by the Maitre d'Hotel, Mr Watson, who was Jamaican and very efficient in his responsibilities. After the meal, the table guests were escorted by the captain to the show lounge where a table had been reserved and waiter solely designated to attend the free drink requirements of the captain's guests, who always took the opportunity to "fill their boots".

For the second sitting evening meal, the Chief Engineer David Lynn and I had separate tables of six passengers each who didn't change from that table for the entire cruise, so we were able to form good relationships and friendships during the cruise.

On embarkation day, we usually sailed at 4 p.m. and had a lifeboat muster with the crew and passengers, to make the passengers familiar with safety procedures, after which the passengers would congregate in the main lounge where the Cruise Director would give a detailed talk concerning the ports of call, tours available, where to shop and the recommended rate of tipping for the waiters, bus boys and cabin stewards, which was $3 per day for waiters and cabin stewards and $2 per day for bus boys. (Bus Boys are the men who clear away the dirty plates from the table.) Where to shop was stressed because the Cruise Director received a "back hander" from the store owners for recommending their shops. The officers had their own personal steward who cleaned their cabin and arranged for their laundry. They gave them a monthly ex gratia payment. I gave Presmey, my cabin steward, who was Haitian, $30 per month.

A daily newsletter was placed in each cabin at night with a schedule of the following day's events and activities. Mostly the ship was scheduled to arrive in port at 6 a.m. and sail at 5 p.m. so that we could coin the cash in from the tours during the day and the bars and casino at night. In the casino on the

Veracruz, the first "one arm bandit" on the right-hand-side of the entrance was "rigged" to pay out more frequently than any other machine because the frequent ringing of bells indicating a jackpot hit seemed to have a hypnotic effect on passengers and drew them into the casino.

The *Veracruz* was a very homely cruise liner and the dress code was casual except for dinner at night when a lounge suit for the men and suitable dress for the ladies was required. A chance to dress-up usually occurred on the second evening out when the Captain had his cocktail party and passengers were introduced to him individually in line by the hostess before they proceeded into the Show Lounge and the ship's photographers had the opportunity to make a "killing" by photographing the individual passenger's introduction to the Captain and the passenger purchasing the photographs at a later date. Most of the passengers purchased the photographs and with 800 passengers, the resulting cash was quite an appreciable amount. The two photographers were employed by the company who had bought the franchise to operate on the ship.

There was also a Captain's private cocktail party for repeat passengers and group escorts, usually during the week in the morning when at sea. At one of these cocktail parties I met an English lady called Ann Barwick who was escorting a large group of passengers. She later married an Indonesian bar manager named Aka Suliaman. Jacqui and I became very good friends of Ann and Aka. When I retired we took six month holidays in Florida, over the winter period of course, and initially rented the condominium of Sylvia Ventigmeglia who was employed on the *Veracruz* as Assistant Purser, but a couple of years later stayed at their home when we became partners together with an American couple in a restaurant venture, but that's a sad story to be told later in this book.

As Staff Captain, I was responsible to Captain Thorne for the overall efficient working of the ship in complying with U.S. Coast Guard and Public Health regulations, also the investigation of any passenger or crew complaints, incidents or accidents and compiling the resulting reports by taking statements of witnesses for the information of the Company's Lawyers. I was also responsible for the general conduct of the crew, issuing fines for any breaches of discipline. I also interviewed applicants whenever a junior position became vacant in the Purser's department, although that was not very often because the girls tended to remain for a number of years on the ship. When we did have a vacancy we usually had our Agent in Montreal place advertisements in the local paper. The girls would send their C.V's and I would reduce the hundreds of applications to about five and interview them in Montreal on the following voyage. Although there was one exception. An English lady called Sylvia Ventimeglia applied for the Assistant Chief Purser's post. She had married an Italian/American but they had recently been divorced and she was starting a new life for herself. She was very smart and presentable and was hired. She eventually became Chief Purser and Sylvia became good friends with my wife Jacqui and I. We still are.

When Captain Thorne went on vacation, which was about twice a year, for a month or so, I superseded him as Captain.

When I first joined the *Veracruz* and commenced my duties as Staff Captain, I thought it would be best to observe the operations of the different departments, then decide in which area I could make improvements without upsetting the various heads of department.

The first observation I made was very early in the morning at about 1 a.m. when the food manager gave me a conducted tour of the catering storerooms, kitchens, dish-wash and dining room areas. All these areas were infested with cockroaches! I immediately commandeered some of the cleaners and headed a swot team to eliminate the little beggars. First of all I sprayed a gas irritant into the crevices where the cockroaches were coming and going from and to. The result was amazing! It was like an invading army, swarms of agitated cockroaches everywhere. Then I sprayed them with a chemical cockroach killer mixture, which made them instantly curl up and die. This operation became a regular weekly exercise and eventually we cleared the infestation. I became known amongst the crew as " The Exterminator".

Occasionally at night, about 10 p.m., accompanied by the bar manager, I did spot checks on the different bar cash tills to ensure all the cash taken in sales had been recorded. I found that some sales had been made but not recorded, the resultant cash being placed under the cash receptacle to be collected at the end of the bartender's shift. Also when comparing bar sales, it appeared that the sales had been drastically reduced compared to previous voyages and on closer examination of the spirit bottles in use, the bottles were not those supplied by our ship chandler. The conclusion was that the bartenders had set up their own little business, purchasing their own spirits and using the ship's facilities to further their own business.

At night I also patrolled the casino area to observe operations. The Filipino girl dealers had a "tip" box and when some of the passengers had a good win, they gave the croupiers a chip. The girls knocked the chip on the table to draw the attention of the casino manager, Lennie, and the players to the fact that the chip was a tip and they were putting it in their "tip" box. I never did catch any of the girls cheating, although that's no guarantee that they didn't. Occasionally, when the casino closed, normally at midnight, I would attend to witness the takings count and the emptying of their "tip" box. There was never a count deficit. We always made money.

Most of the passengers were quite elderly and we often had medical emergencies due to overindulgence in eating, games and dancing. I noticed on these occasions the doctor and nurse, our medical team, were overloaded with all kinds of equipment so I formed an emergency response team of room stewards led by Mr Ham, the Chief Steward, to carry the medical equipment to the site wherever the medical emergency was and transport the passenger back to their cabin or to the hospital for further treatment.

In the Caribbean we had an average of one death every two or three weeks, usually caused by overindulgence resulting in a heart attack. The body was transported to cabin E6 in a special roll of carpeting rather than a body bag so as not to alarm any passengers who may be encountered en route. The body was laid out in the bunk expertly by Mr Ham who held a friendly conversation in a reverent manner with the deceased; then the body was surrounded with packs of ice which were renewed as necessary until we returned to the States where a hearse would be waiting to transport the body to the mortuary. If the deceased had been travelling with a partner they were accommodated in an alternative cabin and they were comforted for the rest of the cruise by the resident priest and cruise staff.

On joining the *Veracruz* I had been assigned the Owner's opulent cabin which attracted the largest rate for passenger occupancy, about $2000 for the 7-day cruise. After a week or so the cabin adjacent to Captain Thorne's, where he had his exercise equipment, was cleared out and it became the Staff Captain's cabin, so I moved in there. The bulkhead separating the two cabins was very thin and Captain Thorne's bedroom was immediately next to the bulkhead. After a couple of sleepless nights with cotton wool stuffed into my ears and a pillow over my head, due to the extra activity noises issuing from Jens' bedroom, I mentioned the fact to Jens. That day, after I had completed my inspections, I returned to my cabin to find Mr Ham with his workforce, securing thick mattresses to the bulkhead. He made such a good job of the alterations that it looked as if the mattresses had always been there. To test if the modifications were successful, Mr Ham went into Jens' bedroom and gave a few high-pitched squeals that were inaudible in my cabin, so the exercise was a great success.

During the morning and afternoon when we were in port, I supervised the working of the deck department, organised drills and kept up with any resulting paperwork.

The crew were exercised at lifeboat and fire drill once a week while in port. The abandon ship signal was sounded on the ship's whistle, the crew mustered at their lifeboat station and those attending checked against the muster list by the officer in charge of the lifeboat. The crew then entered their designated lifeboat and the Captain gave a short blast on the ship's whistle and all the lifeboats on the open water side of the ship were lowered into the water in unison. The crew of the motor lifeboats secured the non-motor lifeboats behind them and towed them around the harbour back to the ship, where they were hoisted up, stowed and the drill completed. The passengers who had elected to remain on board and not go on tours were always quite impressed with the execution and efficiency of the drill and usually greeted the completion with applause.

Fire drill was usually carried out on a different day to the lifeboat drill. The fire bell was sounded; everyone went to their allotted stations. Sprinkler system, engine room shutdown fans and remote stop valves tested. Any passengers remaining on board and walking around inside the ship were escorted to open decks by designated crew.

The areas of passenger ship cruising depend on choosing the time when the weather can be decent, interesting ports of call and embarkation/disembarkation, regarding airport, road and rail access. Choosing Tampa as the embarkation/disembarkation or "home" port met the requirements of access. We called at Playa del Carmen and Cozumel in Mexico and Key West in Florida on our way back to Tampa, meeting the requirements of interesting ports of call and we cruised this itinerary from October to June meeting the requirements of decent weather. This is the best time to cruise because you can expect reasonable weather, not too hot and the hurricane season is petering out.

We departed Tampa on a Saturday afternoon, arriving off Playa del Carmen in Mexico, on a Monday morning, where we had to anchor because the water was too shallow to dock alongside the quay. Small boats called tenders, carrying about 70 passengers, would perform a shuttle service from the *Veracruz* to Playa, where the passengers would then disperse and just laze on the beach or go on tours that had been organised on the ship. The tours varied from visiting Mayan ruins at Chichen Itza, visiting Cancun with its stunning hotels and quaint markets or visiting a national park called Xel-Ha Lagoon, where rare species of fish, turtles and birds abounded.

While we were at anchor, the crewmembers who were off duties would occupy their time in fishing. The amount of fish in that area was prolific, especially large 5-foot specimen of barracuda, which the crew cooked for themselves after testing if the fish was edible. They used to make a cut near the dorsal fin, put a silver dime in the cut, leave it for a while and if it didn't discolour the fish was edible.

The one that didn't get away!

At 5 p.m. we lifted our anchor and proceeded to the Island of Cozumel (which means Island of Swallows). It was only 12 miles from Playa so we were usually all tucked up alongside the quay by 6.30 p.m. Most of the passengers and crew would explore the many bars in the nearest town of San Miguel, but some passengers just stayed on the ship and enjoyed the shipboard entertainment. At the end of the quay where the *Veracruz* berthed was a line of souvenir shops adjacent to a hotel called the Sol Caribe where a special show was put on especially for the passengers, but the drinks were quite expensive.

Due to the swift currents, the waters off Cozumel are so clear that you could see the sandy/coral seabed 100 feet below the water's surface. It is a well-known place for snorkelling or scuba diving. A couple, Jim Ketrow and his partner Jennie Chadina who were dive masters, had the concession before arrival at Cozumel to instruct passengers in the art of scuba diving or snorkelling and to arrange diving tours, for which the company was paid a portion of the cost charged to each participating passenger. Just off the coast an aeroplane lies on the seabed, which is a snorkelling and scuba divers dream to explore. One voyage when my wife Jacqui was with me, we went snorkelling to see the aeroplane and just floated over the wreck, 120 feet below us as clear as day. Out of the corner of my eye I spotted six or seven large barracuda about 30 feet away just hovering and watching us. Jacqui hadn't seen the barracuda and I just motioned to her that we should make our way back to shore. When we arrived on the beach I told Jacqui about the barracuda and she was a bit annoyed that I hadn't pointed them out. I was just relieved that they had not gone for any of our dangling bits.

We departed Cozumel at 6 p.m. on the Tuesday night for Key West, having Wednesday at sea and arriving at Key West at 6 a.m. on the Thursday morning. Key West is the southernmost island of a series of islands running from the Florida mainland which are connected by bridges. A tour of interesting places can be accessed by taking the "Conch Train", which is really a lorry disguised as a train pulling a set of open carriages behind it in which the passengers sit. The tour incorporates visiting Hemingway's house which is now a museum, the late President Trueman's "Little White House" and Sloppy Joe's, a favourite bar of the late Tennessee Williams, where the "Conch Train" passengers alighted to sample the special drinks.

We departed Key West at about 6 p.m. Thursday night witnessing a fabulous sunset, for which phenomenon Key West is well known.

We had Friday at sea, steaming at reduced speed to arrive at the disembarkation port of Tampa at 6 a.m. Saturday morning. On the Friday night we had a passenger talent show prearranged by the Cruise Director who held auditions and it was amazing the amount of musical and other passenger talent on board. Then it was arrival at Tampa, disembarkation, taking on board fresh water, stores, cleaning cabins and public areas before the embarkation procedures and new passengers boarded.

We had a very stringent U.S. Public Health inspection at least once a year but occasionally more frequently. A pass was a total of 85 points. The inspection started with 100 points and for every breach of the Health Regulations, points were deducted. It was very hard to pass the inspection because, for instance, if one of the many refrigerators was not at the minimum temperature, 15 points were deducted. The ship was not banned from sailing for failing the inspection, only if there were chronic Public Health deficiencies. The results of all passenger ship public health inspections are recorded and published in a cruise magazine. It is not surprising famous large passenger ships regularly do not pass, given the stringency of the inspections, the massive areas and equipment involved. After I joined the *Veracruz*, we had a failed inspection before we passed and became one of the elite.

The inspector would board the ship on arrival at 6 a.m., usually in Tampa, observe how the breakfast was being served and dirty crockery taken from the tables. They would observe the kitchen operations; take temperatures of refrigerators and dishwasher temperatures. Inspect for rodents, cockroaches and test the fresh water to ensure the chlorine content was sufficient and a host of other inspections, which usually took about four hours. The Health Inspector was invariably a Mr Yashik, who had in tow, the Staff Captain, Chief Engineer, Hotel Manager, Chief Steward and Bar Manager to write down his comments and items which needed attention. After the inspection Mr Yashik would sit down with the Captain, Staff Captain, Chief Engineer and Hotel Manager to itemize each breach of the Health Regulations and his recommendations.

When we were arriving at the berth in Key West or Tampa, a scan was made of the waiting officials to see if Mr Yashik, the U.S. Public Health inspector, was waiting. If he was, a message was sent over the public address tannoy system for number 001 to report to the bridge. Heads of Departments were informed and panic ensued.

The U.S. Coast Guard made an annual inspection of the ship to ensure the ship complied with safety regulations and had the necessary documents for cruising. The ship's officer's certificates of competency were inspected to verify the ship was manned by competent officers. The charts were inspected to ensure the ship had the charts for the intended voyages and that they were correct and up-to-date. Boat and fire drills were carried out to ensure the crew knew what they were doing in case of emergency. When the inspection had been completed, which took about five hours, a "Letter of Compliance" was issued which indicated the ship had passed inspection to continue its intended trade.

One of the Inspecting Officers, called Richard Hemeon, was married to Brenda, an English lady. Both David Lynn, I and our wives became very good friends with them. Brenda had been a trapeze artist in the Ringling Circus, had a fall and broken both legs and suffered other trauma which curtailed her career. Jacqui and I spent a day with them at the wintering quarters of the Ringling Circus in Sarasota, Florida. We were shown through the train the owners used for transporting the circus from town to town and also used as their living quarters. They were quite luxurious with all mod cons. We were invited to have lunch with the circus artists and their children in a large cafeteria. During the meal the children, aged from 3 to 14 were tumbling and doing balancing acts, starting on the bottom rung of the ladder so to speak.

In 1982, the Filipino Engineer Officer in charge of maintaining the ship's air conditioning units, Rodolfo Ignacio, started giving instructions to the Officers and crew in the art of Tae-Kwon-Do. Rodolfo was a Master Instructor and Black Belter 4th Dan in the art. We utilized the cinema space for the instruction and I eventually attained a 1st Degree Black Belt Certificate, as did most of the pupils. There are 10 patterns. Completing 1 through 4 patterns constitute a blue belt, 1 though 7 constitute a brown belt and 1 through 10 constitute a black belt.

Veracruz Tae-Kwon-Do group. Captain Thorne fifth from the left
top row, me third from the left top row.

Me receiving black belt first dan certificate.

As I mentioned, one of my duties was to investigate accidents, make written reports and take witness statements for the information of the company's lawyers. We had some very interesting, bizarre incidents and accidents.

On one occasion in Tampa when passengers were embarking, I was called to the boat deck where a lady had fallen down some accommodation ladders and hurt her back. When I arrived at the scene, the doctor was in attendance examining the lady, while the lady's husband had a tape measure out measuring the depth of the step and the height of each successive step, photographing the tape measure alongside the step and his wife's injuries. The lady had several wheals on her back which the husband claimed had been caused by the fall. I took statements and suggested that the lady should go to the local hospital for a check-up, but the husband said they had been saving up for this cruise to celebrate their wedding anniversary so they would stay on the ship and our doctor could attend to his wife. I sent my report and supporting photographs to our lawyer the following week. A few weeks later I was informed that the couple were going to sue the company; the case was settled out of court because the spacing of the accommodation ladder steps did not meet legal requirements. Apparently, the ladder was the original ladder when the ship was built, but the regulations concerning the dimensions of the steps had changed since then and had not been picked up by the ship's operators. The lawyer also informed me that the couple appeared to have made a career of going on cruise ships, finding fault in equipment or fittings and having accidents, which were always settled out of court. Our faulty ladders were quickly rectified.

A really bizarre case happened while we were in Mexico. Late one night, Willie Abadan, our doctor, was called to the cabin of a lady who was bleeding profusely from the vagina. She was laid on her blood-soaked bed, in terrible pain; the shower room was also covered in blood. She claimed that she went to the toilet and the steward must have left the toilet brush in the toilet and she had sat on it. She was sent to the local hospital for emergency treatment and we sailed without her. On investigating to compile my report, I questioned the passenger in the adjoining cabin who stated that she had heard an almighty scream, had opened her cabin door in time to see a lady come out of the other cabin who rushed by her. She had gone to the other cabin, realised the situation required immediate medical help and so called the doctor. I did not find out who the mystery lady was. On investigating further, I measured the toilet brush which was 10 inches in length, placed it in the toilet bowl and the top of the toilet brush handle was 5 inches below seat level so it could not have been the brush being left in the toilet by the cabin steward which caused the injury. I had the ships photographers take snaps of the toilet brush against a tape measure; also measured the depth of the toilet bowl from the seat to the base and for good measure had a photograph of Paul Lombardino, our Assistant Cruise Director, sitting on the toilet with the brush placed inside, giving a big smile. I delivered the report to our Lawyers on arrival in Tampa who confirmed they had notice from the lady's lawyers that she was going to sue the ship for injury and trauma due to negligence. Two weeks later the lawyer informed me that the planned action had been cancelled due to my comprehensive report.

Another incident I had to investigate was when a lady passenger claimed that her room steward had tried to rape her. She had run out of her cabin with her blouse torn shouting that the steward had tried to rape her. I immediately interviewed her and took her statement. Then I interviewed the Jamaican steward. He was very frightened, upset and sobbed, "Captain Anderson, I would never do anything like that! She was in the cabin and started screaming and tore her blouse, then ran screaming into the alleyway." I knew the steward quite well and he certainly wouldn't have done anything like that. The lady was allocated another cabin steward and completed the cruise without further problems. I submitted my report to the lawyers on arrival in Tampa. A couple of weeks later they informed me that the lady wanted to settle out of court but he had found out that she had pulled the same stunt on other cruise ships who had settled out of court to avoid bad publicity. He told her that the case would have to go to court and he didn't hear from her again.

The Cruise Line Association occasionally sent confidential information to ships advising them of people, including their photograph in some cases, "doing the rounds" of cruise ships with different scams involving casinos and staged accidents. The casino cheat warnings usually involved "one arm bandit cheats" using magnet arrangements.

During the holiday season, our Caribbean itinerary was changed slightly to a five-day Florida/Mexico cruise, missing out Key West so that we could accommodate a two-day "Cruise to Nowhere". We left Tampa on a Saturday, steamed 12 miles from the coast to comply with American Laws regarding gambling, then stopped engines and just drifted until Monday morning. It was a drinking, gambling cruise and as the cost was only $100 for the two days, it was worth the $100 just for the food, accommodation and entertainment. Where else could you find better value for your money?

As soon as we were 12 miles from the coast, the Casino was open and didn't close except for an hour every 12 hours to empty the overflowing buckets of quarters under the one-armed bandits and clean up the surrounding area. Quite a good deal of liquor was consumed at duty free prices and some passengers did drink more than was good for them.

On one particular "Cruise to Nowhere", I was called at 2 p.m. by the officer on watch who reported that he had received a complaint from a passenger that there was a fracas going on in the adjacent cabin. I collected Mr Ham, my "minder", and went to the cabin in question. Before we arrived we could hear the noise and I thought, no wonder there had been complaints! When I opened the door, a young man in a drunken stupor was standing over a young girl, who was cowering in the corner of the settee, blood streaming down her face, shouting and swearing at her. I asked the young man what the trouble was. He told me to mind my own business, get out of the cabin and took a swing at me. Before I could move, it would have been too late to stop being punched anyway, but Mr Ham had caught his fist, twisted his arm behind his back and smashed his head into the bulkhead (wall) and put handcuffs on him, all in one movement, or so it seemed. The man now had blood streaming down *his* face. We took him struggling to the ship's hospital where the doctor, Willie Abadan, was waiting to stitch him up. I told Willie about the girl and he sent the nurse to attend to her.

The handcuffs were the type which tightens if the person is struggling, and when we arrived at the hospital the man's hands were blue through lack of blood. The man was complaining about his hands and I made him promise that if we removed the cuffs he would behave himself. He agreed and when we removed the cuffs he tried to take another swing at me, resulting in a repeat performance from Mr Ham. Willie wasn't very gentle stitching the wound but the man was drunk enough not to feel any pain. We isolated the man in a special cabin (E6) and put a guard on the door, informing the police of the incident. In the morning, when we arrived back in Tampa, the man was full of remorse but the police were waiting to take him into custody. His girlfriend refused to bring charges and they went off the ship arm in arm, sporting their war wounds, all lovey dovey.

When we arrived in Tampa, the Customs Officers would board to clear the ship and often the drugs squad with dogs that made a thorough search of the ship for drugs accompanied them. On one occasion, after the drugs squad had completed their search and found nothing, one of the cooks had gone ashore carrying a "ghetto blaster" (large radio/cassette player) on his shoulder. He walked, about 15 feet away from one of the drugs quad with his dog and the dog started going crazy. The officer stopped the cook and the dog indicated that the radio contained drugs. The officer examined the "ghetto blaster" and found that there were no working parts inside, only bundles of marijuana. He was taken into custody and eventually sent back to Jamaica.

The chief officer of the drugs squad who always down dressed in ragged, nondescript clothes, which seemed to be the drug squads uniform, was called "Butch" and I became quite friendly with him. One day, after the search, he came to my cabin with a packet of dope he said he had found on the ship. He couldn't find out who had hidden it so he should fine the ship, but because we were friends he wouldn't report it. However, would I do a favour for him? He wanted to plant an agent on the ship as a crewmember to try and find out where the drugs were being obtained. I agreed and a couple of hours later he turned up with this guy in the undercover drug squad uniform of tatty clothes. I pointed out to Butch that the undercover agent would be instantly recognised in that clothing and that he should change into decent jeans and shirt, which he did and was duly engaged as a sailor. The ruse succeeded because Butch was very pleased on our next visit and informed me that they had obtained the information they were looking for.

Our daughter Susan wanted to sail on cruise ships, so I used my influence with the company who had the shop concession to obtain a position for her in the shop, but not on the *Veracruz*. She joined a cruise vessel called the *Emerald Seas* as shop assistant sailing from Miami to the Bahamas. While she was on board there, instead of taking my leave in the U.K., Jacqui and I had a complimentary cruise on the *Emerald Seas*, which, although like a busman's holiday, was a refreshing change to laze around as a passenger. George Reilly, who had been Purser on the *Veracruz* when I joined, had moved on and was Purser on the *Emerald Seas*. I had contacted George to keep his eye on Susan and when we sailed on the *Emerald Seas* he reported that she had been behaving herself and was a popular girl both with the crew and passengers. Susan also served as assistant shop manager on the *Azure*

Seas. She stayed in that job for just over one year. She didn't save any money but had a marvellous time.

In June we changed our itinerary and made New York our "home" port, sailing to New Bedford Massachusetts, which is a fishing port, having a large population of Portuguese/American fishermen, no doubt descendants of seamen engaged in the whaling industry. It was a major whaling port and part of the film, "Moby Dick" was filmed there. The Bethel (Hebrew for House of God) or chapel was where the whalers went to pray before they sailed and is still in use as a nondenominational church. It is part of the New Bedford Whaling National Historical Park. There is a whaling museum opposite the Bethel and the area is a well-known tourist attraction.

Sailing from New Bedford, we transited the Cape Cod Canal to Halifax, Nova Scotia, which is famous for the Halifax Explosion. On December the 6th 1917 the *Mont-Blanc*, a French cargo vessel fully loaded with wartime explosives, collided with a Norwegian vessel called the *Imo* in "The Narrows" section of the Harbour, causing the detonation and huge explosion of the explosives. About 2,000 people were killed by debris, fires and collapsed buildings and about 9,000 people were injured.

Continuing our cruise from Halifax, we circled Bonaventure Island at the entrance of the Saint Lawrence River to view the thousands upon thousands of sea birds that nested there.

We then proceeded up the Saint Lawrence River until we came to the entrance of the Saguenay River, which, due to the fresh water of the Saguenay meeting the salty water of the Saint Lawrence, created an environment suitable for the production of an abundance of krill, making the area very attractive as a feeding spot to beluga and minke whales. We always stopped the engines and drifted for about 30 minutes for the passengers to observe the whales and we were never disappointed. The whales always made their appearance on queue.

Then we continued up the Saguenay Fjord, with stunning scenery until we came to Trinity Bay. On one side of the bay is Cape Eternity and the other side Cape Trinity, towering over 1,100 feet above sea level and dropping vertically into the water so that we were able to enter Trinity Bay and steam only about 100 yards from shore. Near the summit of Cape Trinity was a statue of the

Virgin Mary called Our Lady of the Saguenay. The statue, designed in 1881 by Louis Jobin, is almost 35 feet in height and weighs 3 tons. It was sculpted in solid white pine and sheathed in lead to protect her from the weather. The Cruise Director, Cliff Nelson, gave a running commentary over the public address tannoy system informing the passengers of the age and details of construction as we passed by the statue, then played a recording of Ave Maria, which often brought tears to the eyes of passengers.

Veracruz entering Trinity Bay, top right is the statue of Our Lady of the Saguenay.

Leaving the Saguenay River we proceeded to Quebec. In Quebec, passengers could take tours by horse-drawn carriage to places of interest or have an expensive coffee at the rather classy and expensive Chateau Frontenac Hotel, perched on the top of cliffs called the "Heights of Abraham". The stunning panoramic view from the hotel is worth the price of the coffee. The Heights of Abraham are where, in the war in Canada between France and Britain, in 1759, General Wolfe's soldiers scaled the Heights of Abraham at night and subsequently captured Quebec by surprising the French forces of the Marquis de Montcalm who did not guard that area because they thought the cliffs were insurmountable. There is a designated path from the bottom to the top of the cliffs and if you have plenty of energy to spare, you can take the route the British soldiers took that historic night, although it's much easier taking the reverse route from the top to the bottom.

From Quebec we made our way to Montreal, which was our disembarkation/embarkation point for passengers in Canada. Some of the passengers had booked for a two-week cruise from New York and back to New York, but most had only booked a one-week cruise either New York to Montreal or Montreal to New York. For the benefit of the two-week passengers we arranged some different ports of call on the return cruise from Montreal to New York.

On one passage from Montreal to Quebec, a young man was showing off to his friends at 2 o'clock in the morning, by walking and balancing on the taff rail on the stern of the ship. He slipped and fell into the fast flowing river, which was extremely cold. When the incident was reported to the bridge, Captain Jens Thorne turned the ship around in the narrow channel and dispatched the rescue boat without any hope of recovering the man. It was a miraculous manoeuvre and I am convinced that Jens was the only person who could have done that without damage to the ship in such narrow constraints. It must have been divine intervention because the man was picked up by a fishing boat soon after he had fallen overboard and was transferred to our rescue boat and returned to the ship.

In the morning Jens called the man to his cabin and told him to pack his bags and leave the ship because he had put the passengers and ship in danger by his actions. The man was anything but remorseful and stated his father was a well-known lawyer and he would sue the company. Jens told the man to read the small print on his ticket and he would find out the Captain could do almost anything he wished. The man departed and nothing else was heard from him or his father.

On the return journey to New York from Montreal, we still called at Quebec, went down the Saguenay River, circled Bonaventure Island but called at Sydney, Cape Breton Island.

Sydney has a growing tourist industry, with several nearby attractions, including the Louisbourg Fortress, the Glace Bay Miners Museum, the Alexander Graham Bell Museum and the Cape Breton Highlands National Park, so there was plenty of interesting places for our passengers to visit.

Our agent in Sydney was Tom Sullivan. He and his wife Dot became firm friends with me and the Chief Engineer David Lynn, also Jacqui and Judy, our wives. Dot's forte was reading Tarot Cards. She read my cards saying that I would not remain at sea all my working life, which I didn't, so that was right. She also stated that the ship would have an accident in the Saint Lawrence River but it wouldn't be serious. That was also right because two voyages later, going from Quebec to Montreal, our steering gear failed and we went aground on a mud bank. If we had to go aground that was the ideal place, because either side of that area the seabed was rock. We were really stuck fast and had to wait for high water and call for tug assistance to be released from the mud's suction. We were delayed about nine hours docking at Montreal, which caused mammoth problems for Shirley Peak, our Passenger Liaison Manager and office staff, arranging accommodation and rearranging flights for passengers due to embark and disembark. Fortunately, there was no damage to the ship's bottom, so our cruises continued as normal.

Dot also read David Lynn's cards. She told him that in a few years time he would stop going to sea but he would obtain a position connected with the sea in the Mediterranean. With hindsight that prediction proved to be right as well because some years later David was made redundant when the passenger ship he was serving on, called the *Liberte*, was sold. I was also on the same ship and suffered the same fate.

Consequent to the redundancy, David obtained employment as Marine Superintendent in a passenger ship company called Ocean Cruise Line, based in London, where he remained for five years, after which he obtained employment as Marine Superintendent with a passenger ship company called Unicom Passenger Shipping Line based in Cyprus, where he remained for nine years.

From Sydney, we transited the Cape Cod Canal and called at Fall River, Massachusetts.

Fall River is infamous for the joint murder of Mr Andrew Borden and his wife Abby, allegedly by their daughter Lizzie on August the 4th 1892. Lizzie was arrested and brought to trial but was found not guilty due to insufficient evidence. After that she lived a recluse's life in the family home. During the trial a popular rhyme in circulation was:

> Lizzie Borden took an axe,
> And gave her mother forty whacks,
> When she saw what she had done,
> She gave her father forty-one.

The house is now open to the public as a museum, also a bed and breakfast establishment. You can book Lizzie Borden's bedroom for a restful sleep and have a breakfast similar to the one the Bordens ate on the morning of the murders. How gruesome is that!

There are also numerous clothes factory outlets with great bargains for any shopaholic passengers.

Leaving Fall River, we steamed back to New York to repeat the routine of the disembarkation of mostly satisfied customers and the embarkation of excited, 'can't wait to cruise' passengers.

Late in 1983 Common Brothers acquired another passenger vessel which they named *Bermuda Star*. Jens Thorne was appointed Captain and I became permanent Captain of the *Veracruz* in January 1984. Jens took most of the heads of departments with him, which was natural because he knew he could rely on them to overcome a difficult "settling in" period.

A 6 foot 3 inch tall Swedish Captain called Jan Larsen was appointed Staff Captain on the *Veracruz* and Mark Bernard, Hotel Manager. I formed a good working relationship with both these gentlemen during the time I was on the *Veracruz*.

While on the *Veracruz* I was able to have my wife Jacqui accompany me on numerous occasions. When she did accompany me, I kept her occupied, unpaid, by having her assist the Purser's department in the reception area, especially at embarkation time when all the Purserettes were otherwise occupied. Jacqui bore the brunt of all the new passenger complaints regarding misplaced luggage and unsuitable cabins. Her past experience as a nurse, encountering all kinds of emergencies and developing a good bedside manner, seemed to stand her in good stead as a receptionist.

I remember on one occasion in New York, Jacqui told me that a gentleman had come to the reception area really irate. He had lost his luggage, his cabin was unsuitable and his journey to the ship had been fraught with difficulties. He was making each point by violently wagging his finger and was rather incoherent. Jacqui quietly took hold of his finger and laid it on the counter and in a calm voice asked him to tell her again in a quiet manner and she would do what she could to address his complaints. That seemed to do the trick and Jacqui passed the passenger over to George Reilly, the Purser, who performed his very generous bar credit chit routine and assured the man his complaints would be investigated. The man's luggage was found and, as usual, the complaint regarding the size of the room didn't matter after a few drinks and the difficulties he had experienced joining the ship seemed to have disappeared in an alcoholic haze.

Jacqui gave me the name of the gentleman as well as his cabin number, and I invited him to the Captain's Table. He was so embarrassed when I introduced him to Jacqui as my wife that he apologized profoundly about his conduct. It was a good human behaviour exercise.

On taking command of the *Veracruz*, I appointed a crew committee to discuss any problems brought to their attention which could be dealt with internally and, if not, to bring officially to my attention. Also, how the fines collected from wayward crewmembers could be spent for the benefit of all crewmembers, such as T.V.'s, washing machines, etc. This action proved an instant success with everyone.

I also made a special purchase of an 18-carat gold 'number one' from the jeweller's recommended by Cliff Nelson, Cruise Director, in Key West, obtaining a good discount, of course. Each week, the heads of department recommended an outstanding employee of the week, usually a waiter or room steward, and the gold number one was presented to the employee at the Captain's Passenger Cocktail Party. I made quite an event of the presentation, pinning the gold number one onto their uniform and remarking to the passengers that they were very lucky if they had the services of the number one employee that week. The effect of being named the number one employee of the week seemed to attract additional tips, so everyone, especially the waiters, were on their toes trying to be chosen the number one for the following week.

I also initiated a weekly "Man Overboard" exercise on a Friday morning when we were going from Key West to Tampa. At 10 a.m. a lifebuoy with smoke flare attached was thrown into the sea over the stern. As soon as the lifebuoy hit the water the smoke flare was activated by the action of the salt water, giving off a plume of thick smoke. "Man Overboard!" was announced over the tannoy system and the rescue boat crew dashed to prepare the rescue boat for launching; extra lookouts were posted on the bridge and a manoeuvre called "The Williamson Turn" was performed. That involved keeping the vessel at full speed, putting the steering wheel hard over to port or starboard, whichever side the buoy representing the person who had fallen overboard had been released, until the vessel was 60 degrees off course, then putting the steering wheel hard over to the opposite side until the ship's heading was 20 degrees short of the opposite course; then the steering wheel was put to the amidships position and ship brought to the reciprocal course and speed reduced. At that point the smoke plume should be sighted dead ahead. The engines were stopped, the rescue boat dispatched and lifebuoy picked up. The rescue boat returned to the ship and was hoisted back onto the ship to the accompanying applause of the passengers. The whole operation, from the man overboard shouts to the rescue boat being housed back on the ship, only took about 20 minutes.

From left to right, David Lynn Chief Engineer, Costa 1st Engineer, me & Jan Larsen Staff Captain.

Every year, when we were changing our itinerary from New York to Tampa or vice versa, we always called into Norfolk, Virginia to drydock at the Norfolk Shipbuilding and Drydock Corporation. The purpose for drydocking was to have the vessel's underwater area scraped and painted with anti-fouling paint to restrict marine mollusc growth on the hull and overhaul the underwater inlet valves. The opportunity was also taken to paint the ship's hull above the waterline and perform any surveys due for renewal as required by the country of registry and the insurance underwriters.

On the 30th of September 1984, we drydocked in Norfolk Shipbuilding and Drydock Corporation's floating dock. The floating dock consisted of five sections of "U"-shaped structures about 100 feet wide by 100 long by 60 feet high, each leg of the watertight "U" shape being about 50 feet thick. Each section was connected together with heavy chains. Water was pumped into each section until it was deep enough for a vessel to enter the dock. When the ship was in position, the water was pumped out of the "U"-shaped sections simultaneously and so the vessel was "lifted" out of the water by the buoyancy of the structures and landing on special blocks on the bottom of the dock.

At about 3.35 a.m. on the morning of the 1st Of October 1984, I woke up being thrown out of my bed. The ship had fallen violently to starboard to an angle of about 35 degrees. Due to the inclination of the ship, I had difficulty keeping my feet and had to crawl from my cabin along the alleyway to the navigation bridge. The ship had come up against the wall of the floating dock and reposed at an angle of 47 degrees. I crawled to the wing of the bridge and saw crewmembers exiting via the gangway. I saw one crewmember who was going to jump from the ship to the dock and shouted at him to use the gangway, which he did. Some of the crew were lowering themselves onto the dockside by the starboard lifeboat man-ropes, which I did. When I arrived on the dockside I instructed the Hotel Manager, Mark Bernard, to take a head count and see how many were missing. Then I went back on the ship and, accompanied by David Lynn, Chief Engineer and Jan Larsen, Staff Captain, we went into the crew accommodation, shouting and looking for crewmembers. On our way to the crew accommodation I came across the Assistant Purser, Sylvia Ventimeglia, who had hurt her ankle. One of the cooks was helping her and I told them to get on deck, go ashore and report to Mark Bernard.

Continuing with our search, we came across Avery Darling, a Jamaican room steward, who was lying unconscious in the crew accommodation alleyway with head injuries. We carried Avery up onto the open deck where he was placed in a skip and a shore crane lifted him from the ship to the shore where one of many ambulances was commandeered to transport him to hospital as an urgent medical case.

While we had been down in the accommodation searching for crewmembers, the dockyard personnel had pumped water into the "U"-shaped structures until the *Veracruz* was afloat and had come to a 11-degree starboard angle of repose. All kinds of emergency response organisations were now attending, the police, coast guard, ambulance services, and paramedics, and there were even lawyers touting for any prospective business from injured clients.

Thirty-one injured crewmembers were ferried by ambulances to three different hospitals. Their injuries were mainly slight; they were treated in hospital and released. Unfortunately, Avery died from his injuries about four days later.

By light of day, the serious damage to the ship and floating dock was obvious, also inside the ship; due to the violent starboard lurch, tables, chairs, pianos, stores and personal effects had been displaced and lay in a jumbled heap on the starboard side of the ship or starboard side of cabins.

The exhaustive task of recording all the damage to the ship for insurance claim purposes commenced, including crew claims for personnel loss. I asked all crewmembers to make a detailed list of their losses. When they presented their claims they were mind boggling—gold coins and other jewellery they had lost, damaged expensive ghetto blasters—so I asked each person to bring the items they were claiming for to me for verification and evidence for the underwriters. Most of the claimants then seemed to have made a mistake and the losses were not so great.

The incident seemed to have been caused by the leakage of seawater into one of the "U"-shaped constructions, so causing the structure to sink and reduce the supporting buoyancy afforded to the *Veracruz*, resulting in the catastrophic accident.

We went into a much larger drydock for repairs, which took about six weeks and then we sailed to Tampa, Florida, to continue our cruising itinerary.

Of course, there were legal implications resulting from this accident, as to who was responsible and shoulder the enormous costs involved. Our company engaged a legal company called Seawell, Dalton, Hughes and Timms, who assigned a lawyer called Phil Davey, an expert in marine law. I had to attend a meeting in Norfolk on March the 18th 1985, to make a deposition upon oral examination, which was quite an ordeal. David Lynn also had to give a deposition. The case was due to be heard in court later in the year and David had to attend, but the day the case was due to be heard, Norfolk Shipbuilding agreed to settle out of court. Both David and I became good friends with Phil Davey and remained in contact with Phil and his family for some time. I think David is still in contact at Christmas. Phil opened his own practice later and I'm sure is very successful and well known due to his marine legal knowledge and experience.

During one of the Caribbean Cruises, the Company engaged a Television company to film a promotional videotape. I was supposed to invite Travel Agents and prospective passengers at various locations in the U.K. to view the film while I was on vacation. This idea did not materialize because I left the Company before the concept could be acted upon.

In 1985 David Lynn was head hunted by the American Hawaii Cruise Line to take up a position as Chief Engineer on a cruise ship called the *Liberte*, under the Panamanian flag, which was being refurbished in Japan with the intended cruising area being the Polynesian Islands, so he resigned from the Bahama Cruise Line. A few months later he called me and gave me a telephone contact number to ring in case I was interested in the Captain's position… Polynesia! Of course I was interested, so I rang the number.

David must have given a glowing report to the powers that be about me, because I was immediately put through to a Captain Riconni, Operations Vice President, American Hawaii Cruise Lines. He offered me an initial position as Staff Captain for a probationary period of three months, after which I would be promoted to permanent Captain. I accepted the offer and resigned by position with the Bahama Cruise Line, which didn't go down too well with management but the Staff Captain, Jan Larsen, was thrilled to bits because he became Captain of the *Veracruz*.

I left the *Veracruz* in New York and travelled to Sasebo in Japan via Honolulu, where the main office of the American Hawaii Cruise Line was situated, to be interviewed by Captain Riconni and introduced to the office staff.

After a couple of days in Honolulu making myself conversant with the operations and resulting paperwork of the company, I was booked on a flight to Japan to begin my *Liberte* and Polynesian experience.

Chapter Seven

Passenger Ship Captain Years

S.S. Liberte

WHEN I ARRIVED AT SASEBO AIRPORT, I was met by the Agent who guided me through all the Immigration and Customs formalities, then whisked me away by private car to the ship, where David Lynn greeted me like a long lost brother because we were the only English people on board. The Captain, deck and engine room officers were American and crew Filipino. There was only a skeleton crew on board, because after completion of the refurbishment, the ship was programmed to sail to Honolulu, take on the remainder of the crew and stores, then proceed to Tahiti to cruise between the Polynesian Islands.

SS Liberte at anchor, Huahine.

David had been in Sasebo about nine months, supervising the engine and auxiliary machinery refurbishments.

I started familiarizing myself with the layout and compiling a safety handbook for the *Liberte*, which was required to comply with International Regulations. This was an exhaustive task, which I suspect had been purposely left for me to compile and organise.

The *Liberte* was built by Ingalls Shipyards, Pascagoula, Mississippi, U.S.A. in 1958 for Moore-McCormack Lines and was named the *Brasil*. Built originally as a luxury ocean liner to carry 300 passengers and cargo, she had undergone several refurbishments, change of name and Owners, until on completion of refurbishment in Sasebo she was a total passenger cruise vessel, able to carry 800 passengers and 350 crew, quite a high percentage of crew to passenger ratio. She was refurbished to a very high standard. Some luxury suites were spacious, opulent cabins with T.V.'s, direct dialling telephones, safes, luxury furnishings and the en-suite bathrooms had a jacuzzi bath. Two large tender boats, carrying about 70 passengers each, had also been added to the lifeboat capacity because in the intended Polynesian schedule, we had to anchor in three of the ports of call and would have to use our own means of tendering the passengers from the ship to shore and shore to ship.

About one month after I joined, the *Liberte* had completed her refurbishment. The Captain, Cal Bourke, had flown back home to California for a spot of leave and I was going to take over command and take the *Liberte* to Honolulu. Unfortunately, the shipbuilding yard had not been paid for the refurbishment so we did not get a clearance to sail immediately. After a week or so of negotiations between the owners and shipyard, the *Liberte* was given clearance to sail and our voyage to Honolulu commenced.

I hadn't been feeling very well for some time and after a couple of days at sea I was diagnosed by the nurse as having a perforated ulcer. I was laid up in the ship's hospital but managed to visit the navigation bridge a couple of times each day to check on the ship's progress and report our position to head office. The Officers advised me to divert to Wake Island for medical attention but I insisted that we continue our passage to Honolulu. On arrival at Honolulu I was immediately taken off the ship and hospitalised.

My haemoglobin count was 6.3 but due to the nurse's attention and medications, the bleeding had stopped. I received four units of blood in the Honolulu hospital and was discharged after four days, just in time to join the *Liberte* before she sailed for Papeete in Tahiti. On the last day before we sailed, over 1,000 tons of stores had been delivered and the crew were working all night sorting out the stores and securing the ship for sailing the next morning.

The American Hawaii Cruise Line had two other passenger vessels, the Independence and Constitution, registered in the U.S.A. with an all American crew. When the company had purchased the *Liberte*, they had recruited Entertainers, Pursers, Deck and Engine Room Officers, bar and cabin staff from their own vessels to man the *Liberte*. Apparently, it seemed that everyone volunteered for the chance to sail in the Polynesian region.

Off we sailed to Tahiti to begin our French Polynesian experience with a ship full of stores, fully crewed but no passengers. The time taken to reach Papeete, Tahiti, from Honolulu was utilized in making the passenger accommodation and areas spotless, familiarizing the crew with safety aspects of the ship and having drills.

Majority of the Crew pictured on the Poop deck of the *SS Liberte*, moored at Papeete.

The ship was planned to be on a weekly schedule sailing on a Saturday evening from Papeete to Rangiroa, Huahine, Raiatea, Bora-Bora, Moorea, back at Papeete on Saturday morning to disembark passengers. Passengers would embark at 4 p.m. and we would sail again at 11 p.m. Saturday evening. We had to have a local French pilot for each island so the best plan was to take a pilot on the cruise and be available 24 hours per day. The pilot navigated the island channels due to his local knowledge and the captain docked and anchored the ship because of his knowledge of how the ship would respond when manoeuvring. We had two regular pilots, who took weekly turns, Daniel and Pierre. They both enjoyed the relaxed cruising life and I always introduced them to the passengers at the Captain's Cocktail Party.

Introducing Daniel our Pilot at the Captain's Cocktail Party.

All our stores were shipped to us by air from Los Angeles along with the passengers but we did buy some local produce, fresh vegetables, fruit and fish.

Papeete, Tahiti, is the administrative capital of French Polynesia and Tahiti, an island, has about two thirds of the total population with 80,000 people. Papeete is the lifeline of that area, handling virtually all imports as well as inter-island trade and also has the main airport. There are several large quays where all types of vessels, including yachts, berth and now constitute a "must" port of call for cruise ships in that area. The local market, restaurants, rows of shops and jewellery shops selling black pearls are features to capture the attention of tourists.

Rangiroa is a very large atoll, 42 miles long by 16 miles wide. An atoll is a ring shaped coral reef enclosing a lagoon, the sandy land on the coral reef being only tens of feet above sea level. The entrance for large vessels to the lagoon is through the Avatoru Pass which can only be transited for about 30 minutes every slack water between ebb and flood tide—that's four times, sometimes three times per day, because the current after slack water is too strong, reaching speeds of ten knots. The company had buoyed the passage into the lagoon and as far as I know, we were the first cruise ship to visit Rangiroa. The times of arrival and departure varied because slack water varied and we anchored in the lagoon and tendered the passengers ashore and back to the ship.

Calling at Rangiroa was cancelled after a few visits because in the season of the strong trade winds, which blew across Avatoru Pass, entrance was impossible and attempts to enter had to be aborted. I drew the attention of the passengers to the effect of the wind on approaching the pass by making a dummy run and they were disappointed in missing the Rangiroa call but after witnessing the dangers involved they understood my position, which was the point of the exercise.

Huahine is an island with a series of lagoons. It has many archaeological sites and a museum full of Polynesian artefacts which was free for passengers to browse around. There was no quay, so the vessel anchored in a lagoon and tendered the passengers to and from shore. On one occasion, shortly after leaving Huahine, we headed into a typhoon which had been named IRMA (the ninth typhoon of the season) and circled the island keeping in the lee until the typhoon had passed. One of the passengers, Dick Locker, creator of the fictional detective character 'Dick Tracy', sent me a note and drawing to commemorate the occasion.

Raiatea is a large island surrounded by a coral reef with several passes through the reef. The island had a quay so we could berth alongside. There were several places of interest for the passengers to visit, fine restaurants and clubs. There was also a football field, where, after we became established on our schedule and had formed a football team, we played matches against local teams. They played in their bare feet, were rough and tough, if they came to tackle, you gave them the ball. We never did win a match but it promoted a good relationship with the local populous.

Football Team with Cheer Leaders.

Bora-Bora is a large island with two smaller islands, Toopua and Toopua Iti. nearby, the three islands being encircled by a perfect barrier reef, which is only broken once by the Teavanui Pass, through which we proceeded and came to anchor off Bora-Bora. From 1942 to 1946 the island became an American naval base with a garrison of 6,000 men. The musical show "South Pacific" is about the antics of the garrison during that period in Bora-Bora, though I believe the film version of the show was filmed in Bali.

There were plenty of interesting places and restaurants for passengers to visit. One of the tours available was the shark feeding tour which I also experienced. At a set time, about noon, the passengers were loaded into local built canoes, taken out to the edge of the coral reef where white tipped reef sharks could be located. A line was strung between two canoes and all the passengers, fitted with snorkelling masks, jumped into the water. The passengers had to grab hold of the line and the guides smacked the water surface and pretty soon the white tips started appearing. The sharks were fed with fish and when they got in a feeding frenzy the guides ushered us back to the canoes in double quick time. It was quite exciting because although white tips are not considered dangerous, in the feeding frenzy they could have mistaken our arms or legs for juicy tit-bits.

Moorea is a large Island, only about ten miles from Papeete, and has two bays, Cook and Opunoho bays. A barrier reef surrounds the island with many deep-water channels, making access to the island by large vessels possible. Moorea has a population of about 7,000 and is very tourist orientated, having hotels, restaurants, transport rentals, organised island tours and water sports. There is no deep-water quay so we had to anchor in Cook's Bay and tender our passengers to and from shore.

The first few weekly cruises were a bit chaotic, due mainly to new personnel getting accustomed to the ship and their responsibilities, the passenger comment cards reflecting this. The passengers were requested to fill out a comment card at the end of the cruise giving a score for Area of Cruising, Entertainment, Service, Food and Congeniality of the Crew; the score slowly improved each successive week, until finally we were topping the passenger cruise satisfaction league of the American Hawaii Cruises three ships. As an incentive, the company donated to the ship's crew recreation fund, $0.50 per guest for a score of 3.59, $1.00 for a score of 3.75 and $2.00 for a score of

3.90, based on a perfect score of 4. None of the ships ever reached a perfect score but we achieved a score of over 3.75 approaching 3.90 several times.

After about a month, instead of the three-month probationary period, Captain Riconni must have thought I was suitable to take command, and so Captain Bourke went home to California and I was promoted from Staff Captain to Captain. My replacement as Staff Captain was Captain Renato Piovano, an Italian, who had served on Carnival cruise vessels. He was about 40 years old, very smart, efficient, and an excellent artist. We had a very good working relationship which proved successful.

I organised a weekly meeting between Heads of Department and myself to record and endeavour to resolve any outstanding problems they had encountered, and also evaluate the passenger comment cards from the previous week. Any adverse comments were considered and, if valid, how they could be rectified; also any outstanding services they had experienced from the crew and had mentioned on the comment card were considered, with possible ways of being brought to the attention of the individuals concerned.

I also introduced the 'Outstanding Crewmember of the Week' policy, which I had initiated on the *Veracruz* with some degree of success, and its success, in turn, was reflected in the eagerness of the *Liberte*'s crewmembers to be presented to the passengers as Crew Member of the Week.

The Captain's Cocktail Party was one of the high points on a Sunday evening while the vessel was at sea. I changed the format which I adopted on the *Veracruz* and after each passenger had been introduced to me by the Hostess Beth Herich and the passengers were settled in the lounge with their free drinks, I introduced the Crew Member of the Week and in addition all the heads of departments.

Introducing the 'Outstanding Crew Member of the Week' at the Captain's Cocktail Party. Chief Steward Patrick fourth from the left.

After I performed the introductions I gave a brief outline of our itinerary and usually ended the speech with a corny joke about my memory and the passengers being safe in my hands because when I went on the bridge I had my memory jogger with me. In my pocket I had a piece of paper with the words 'right is starboard, left is port'! I would then show the paper to one of the heads of department and ask if it was true, and of course they always said yes but the piece of paper would have a different story on it. I would learn some spicy information about the person I chose to show the paper too and get their confirmation. For instance, on one occasion, there was a story going about that the Chief Steward had formed a relationship with one of the tour staff and I had written on the paper, "Is it true that Dana's knickers are deep purple?" Patrick's eyes boggled, his face went a bright red and he managed to squeak out a strangled… "YES."

On another occasion, Conrad Kuiken, the Cief Officer, had just returned to the ship from vacation. When I introduced Conrad, I explained that he had just returned and while on vacation had auditioned for a singing part in a show because he had an exceptional voice. Would the passengers like to hear Conrad sing? Of course they all shouted yes! Conrad had gone very red faced and was saying, "No, no!" but the more he said no the more the passengers shouted yes! So I suggested to Conrad, as a kind of Captain's Command, he should sing my favourite song, "New York, New York." With great reluctance Conrad agreed and went into his off-tune routine. After he had finished, the passengers gave him some sympathetic applause for trying. "Now you can see why Conrad's back on the *Liberte,*" I remarked. The next week before the Captain's Cocktail Party, Conrad asked me to keep the audition story and him singing in the Cocktail Party presentation, and I agreed. When I introduced the Heads of Department and related the story about Conrad's audition while on vacation and requested him to do his rendering of "New York, New York", I was very surprised because he wasn't reluctant at all and off he went: "Start spreading the news, I'm leaving today... etc."—much to my surprise, in a beautiful voice, which sounded very much like the cruise director's singing voice. They had turned the joke back on me by having the microphone relayed to the cruise director and Conrad just miming! This time when Conrad had finished, the passengers' applause was deafening and they wanted him to sing more. I explained to the passengers that I had played a joke on Conrad the previous week but had it been returned with interest this week, then introduced the real singer.

Captain's Cocktail Party, introducing the Officers. David Lynn Chief Engineer far left, Conrad Kuiken Chief Officer (the singer) third from left.

Another time, I almost caused a mutiny by the heads of departments because of my warped sense of humour. I sent an Interoffice Memorandum to all

Heads of Departments with the subject 'Captain's Cocktail Party Choral Choir', stating:

"To close the presentation at the Captain's Cocktail Party on a Sunday, I think a different format is required. I am proposing a choir or group (groupies) as follows:

Song:	*New York - New York*
Lead Singer:	Mercades
Backing Group:	Staff Captain, Hotel Manager, Chief Engineer and Chief Purser with Doctor and Maitre D' in reserve, singing *Da-da-de-do* several times, interchanged with *de-de-do-da.*

Or, alternatively, the lead singer could be the Staff Captain and Hotel Manager singing *New York - New York* in Italian and the backing group singing *si-si-mama-mia* in time to the music.

For effect, I proposed that "dry ice could be put on the dance floor and Barbara, June and Sharon could flitter around the dance floor lifting their arms up and down slowly, with a slack wrist, which would give the effect of moonies in the fog in New York." I added: "I would like some feedback/comments from the officers so that the cruise director can arrange with the band for rehearsals. Your usual co-operation is anticipated and I'm sure the result will be stunning."

The resulting comments were, as I anticipated, especially from the proposed slack-wristed moonies: "I'm not doing that! Not even for the Captain, not even if I get the sack!" I suspect they all knew it was a joke and were just humouring me with their reactions.

Some crewmembers had duel responsibilities; for instance, my Hostess, Beth Herich, besides introducing the passengers to me at the Cocktail Party, was in charge of children's activities. In collusion with the Cruise Director, she asked me to hold a children's "Coke Tail Party" at 4.30 p.m. prior to the Captain's Cocktail Party, to which I reluctantly agreed. On a previous cruise, I had been intrigued by a magician who had been employed to perform close up "magic" during the evening meal going from table to table. I had the "magician" show me some of his stock tricks and became quite adept in the art. This stood me in good stead to entertain the children at the "Coke Tail Party" because children love to see a bit of "magic". I was going through my "magic" routine on one occasion when one of the little guests, about seven years old, said, "I know how to do that trick!" "That's good," I replied, and every trick I performed, the little angel repeated the same thing. It reached the point when I said between clenched teeth, "Okay, let's see you do *this* one!"

But he performed the trick like a professional, much better than I could have, so I let him finish the entertainment part of the party and gave him a grand tour of the ship as a reward and we became firm friends.

Beth Herich introducing passengers to me at the Captain's Cocktail Party.

I instigated an informal cocktail party on a Friday at 4.30 p.m. for those crewmembers who were proceeding on leave, to show my appreciation for their contribution to the passengers' cruise enjoyment. This event proved very popular and was looked forward to by departing crewmembers.

The fine system which I had introduced on the *Veracruz* I implemented again, whereby any breaches of discipline or rules, such as neglect of duty, being absent from lifeboat drill or late from shore leave would result in fines varying from $5 to $25. The resulting fines were accumulated in a "fine" fund for the use of the crew's recreation activities.

In American registered vessels there was no crew bars or drink allowed but on the *Liberte,* being Panamanian registered, there was a recreation area and the crew were allowed alcoholic drinks. I had the crew form a committee to oversee the running of the crew bar and recreation activities, which worked very well. I attended crew committee meetings when requested, to give my consent to proposed activities and also give my consent to the release of money from the "fine" fund for any sports equipment requisitions, such as football or basketball strips and balls.

One of the activities planned was that one evening, on successive weeks, each nationality of the crew would give a typical presentation in story/play form of their country's history/music. The shop manager, Howard, who was English, wrote a play about King George III involving Beau Brummell. He inveigled me into playing the part of Beau Brummell, which went down very well with the crew. The Filipinos performed a musical evening incorporating the famous bamboo dance and the Americans did a musical evening, but the English evening was voted the best entertainment.

Howard, English Shop Manager as King George III, me as Beau Brummell.

At a crew committee meeting, one of the American room stewards, Drew Farion. asked me if he could start publishing a weekly *Crews News* paper, which I sanctioned, so long as it was all done in his own time and I could scan the material for approval before it was published. This proved to be an inspirational decision; it kept me in touch with what was going on around the ship and the crews' antics ashore. I submitted a weekly item which I entitled, "From The Captain's Sea Chest." It was the vehicle to make the crew aware of how the *Liberte* was performing and also warn all the crew about the consequences of any unsavoury happenings, either on the ship or ashore, which had been brought to my attention. Drew also used the paper to warn the crew regarding the consequences of taking advantage of crew concessions, such as bad behaviour caused by overindulgence.

Every day, there was a passenger keep fit class which was run by one of the very fit cruise staff, but on a Thursday morning I led the group which proved very popular and seemed to attract the most participants. It also kept me fit!

Leading the exercise class.

I still kept up my tonsorial operations (barbering), cutting the officers' hair. One day we had just come to anchor in Bora-Bora and I was cutting David Lynn's hair on the wing of the bridge observed by some passengers. A lady said, "Can you give my husband a haircut? He needs one badly!" I agreed, plonked him down in the seat and gave him a haircut, took an American dollar, wrote my signature on it and gave it to the gentleman. When he asked what the dollar was for I explained that if he wasn't satisfied with the result he couldn't sue me because I had paid him and he had accepted the dollar. Giving passengers a haircut became quite well known and a regular routine, due to the reporting in the *Los Angeles Times* by Stan Delaplane, a recipient of my tonsorial expertise.

Tonsorial operations at a bargain price.

At night, from 8 p.m. to midnight, a disco was held in "Le Club", a smaller, compact ballroom. Occasionally, I was the guest D.J. and introduced the American passengers to the English spot prize, whereby I stopped the music, turned my back to the dancers and issued instructions to my assistant D.J. starting from the centre of the dance floor to take three steps forward, two steps to the side and touch the nearest couple on his left or right. The couple chosen received either a silver bookmark or bottle of champagne as a prize. Most chose the silver bookmark embossed with the AHC line logo. The disco was always well attended. As the dancers got the idea of the spot prize they would try to move to be selected, but this was soon stopped by my assistant D.J.

The company gave me a list of V.I.P. passengers to be given preferential treatment and invited to the Captain's Table for an evening meal during the cruise. There usually wasn't sufficient passengers on the list to cover the whole week, so I invited my own guests. On a Saturday, in Papeete, a buffet meal was served at 6 p.m. to embarking guests and I joined the queue in the guise of a passenger. Taking my meal, I would sit at a table with a number of people and engage them in conversation as to how the trip from San Francisco was and if they had any complaints regarding arrangements made by the company. I would also ask where they were situated on the ship and they would invariably give their cabin number and give a glowing report on the cleanliness and attentive service by the room steward. I would mentally note the cabin number and later in the cruise invite them to my table. It was also a means of hearing first hand any complaints or difficulties they had experienced and informing the powers that be so that the problems could be rectified.

On one occasion, my buffet routine was misunderstood. I had chosen a table where only one sweet old lady was sitting. When I engaged her in conversation, she didn't volunteer her cabin number so I asked her, at which she turned to a neighbouring table where apparently her son with his family was sitting and exclaimed, "This man is coming on and asked me my cabin number!" I had to go to the son and explain in a quiet voice who I was and the reason for wanting his mum's cabin number. "It's okay," the son explained to his mum, "he's only making conversation." The son gave me his mum's cabin number and later in the cruise she received a lovely embossed and fringed with gold invite under her cabin door. I should imagine she kept it as a memento of the cruise and the eccentric captain. It's amazing that not many of the people I met in my passenger guise buffet routine recognised me in my uniform and I had to relate the incident when they came to the table.

Some passengers thought they could be married by the Captain, which is not the case, unless the ship has a license for marriages and the Captain is ordained, which I doubt any are. However, I had several requests to perform a marriage ceremony, which I did on the understanding and it was noted in the certificate, that they legalized the marriage when they returned home. On such occasions, the chef baked a lovely cake and I provided the champagne free of charge to the couple. It was a solemn, yet very happy ceremony, witnessed by many passengers. "Renewal of Marriage Vows" also became a popular occasion with the cake and champagne accompaniment. I understand that legal marriage and renewal of vows ceremonies are available on some passenger vessels now.

I lost my wristlet watch Jacqui had given for my birthday a couple of years previously. The strap must have broken and I believe I lost it in one of the ship's elevators. I made it known to the crew but it was never found. A couple of months later, when I was due to go on leave, the crew held an impromptu party and presented me with a Cartier Parie gold watch, which I still have.

On the 19th April 1986, I was relieved by Captain Cal Bourke to proceed on vacation. On my scheduled return to the *Liberte* six weeks later, I had a detour via Honolulu to join, as a passenger, the *Independence* and cruise the Hawaiian Islands to observe how the American side of things operated. Half way through the cruise I received an urgent message from Head Office to return to the *Liberte* as soon as possible because whilst leaving Raiatea the ship had damaged her starboard propeller on a coral reef. I returned to Papeete post haste and was greeted at the airport by Captain Bourke. It appeared that when the *Liberte* had departed Raiatea at 11 p.m., a critical turn in the channel had been negotiated rather late and the starboard propeller had just caught the edge of the coral reef, bending the blades of the propeller and snapping off the tips. Captain Bourke was scheduled to fly out of Papeete that night but offered to stay and assist me with the paperwork and formalities involved in obtaining a certificate from the underwriter's surveyor to "Carry on Cruising". It would have been no help to have two Captains involved so I declined the offer and Captain Bourke flew out of Papeete that night. The upshot of the accident was that the surveyor issued a certificate for the *Liberte* to proceed on the understanding that the starboard engine would only be used in a dire emergency. This meant that the *Liberte* could be propelled by the port engine only, making manoeuvring more difficult but we were able to maintain our schedule.

A dire emergency occurred one time when we were anchored in Cook's Bay at Moorea. A local gale force wind, when conditions are compatible, occasionally blows down or up Cook's Bay, depending on the season. In the dry season it's called the Mara Amu, which blows from a South Westerly direction up Cook's

Bay and in the wet season it is called the Toerau and blows from a North Easterly direction down Cook's Bay. At this time it was the wet season.

The Toerau started blowing at about 4 p.m. one Friday and the tenders were still bringing passengers back from the shore. At 6 p.m. all the passengers were back on board; we were heading into the wind, lifted the anchor, manoeuvred the ship to turn round with one main propeller, stern and bow thrust propellers and headed towards the exit channel. Before we arrived there, the ship was proving very difficult to control due to only having one propeller in action because over a certain speed the bow and stern thrust propellers are not very effective, so I advised the engine room that we may require to use the damaged propeller. An apparent impending disaster seemed to freeze the pilot's judgement. I took over conning the ship, dropped the starboard anchor and steamed around the anchor. The ship was "brought up" and again heading into the wind. We were about 100 metres from the reef. I heaved up the anchor and proceeded back to our anchorage where we were all through the night steaming at dead slow ahead to maintain our position because the wind was blowing so strong. At daylight the wind eased and we proceeded on our way to Tahiti. Most of the passengers were unaware that we had come so close to a calamity but we had a local reporter on board and the pilot gave him an interview singing my praises of how I had acted and averted a catastrophe, which appeared in the local paper the next day. When a ship has an accident, the captain bears responsibility because pilots are only there to give advice. Knowing when to intervene, when a ship is under the direction of a pilot and the situation is getting out of hand is due to experience and knowledge of the ship's reaction to manoeuvring. On numerous occasions I have had to intervene in the pilot's actions but the Cook's Bay incident was the hairiest ever.

On subsequent visits to Raiatea, after the damage to the starboard propeller, one of the American cooks who was an expert scuba diver and was instructing other crew members in the art, took his protégées to the coral reef, scene of the accident and salvaged the bronze propeller tips which had been broken off. These, he fashioned into ashtrays and sold to crewmembers as mementos.

A terrible accident occurred to one of his protégées. One of the shop assistants, a young American boy, who was also a member of the soccer team, while diving, ran out of air and unfortunately died by drowning as a result. His body was landed and transported back to the States. We had a short commemorative service on the poop deck leaving Raiatea. Writing to advise his parents how the accident had occurred was the hardest letter I have ever had to write. What can you say to parents that will ease the pain of losing a beloved son? I could only relate how he had lost his life in an accident following a sport he was besotted with; and how he will be missed by all his friends on the ship. Being so popular, he had many friends. He was such a nice young man and enjoyed every minute both at work and play on the *Liberte*. The crew held a collection, which raised over two thousand dollars to give to his parents. The parents later informed me that they had donated the collection to his former school for them to buy a suitable commemorative plaque.

Every year, later in his life, Bob Hope recorded a NBC Television winter special programme. On November the 7th 1986 he boarded the *Liberte* while we were anchored at Moorea in Cook's Bay, to tape part of his Winter Tahiti Special, which was televised in February 1987. Mr Hope was accompanied by his wife Delores, Jonathan Winters, Howard Keel, John Denver, Morgan Brittany and Miss America 1986 Susan Akin. Mr Hope was offered an American Hawaii Cruises hat and Christian Dior "T"-shirt embossed with the AHC logo and name *S.S. Liberte* but he declined them. I suppose it broached sponsorship regulations. I didn't mind because I claimed them and still have them. Mr Hope and party were allocated two luxury cabins as changing rooms for the day.

Presenting Bob Hope with a souvenir flag made by Staff Captain Renato Piovano. AHC President Conrad Everhard far right.

Filming commenced at about 4.30 p.m. and was completed by about 6 p.m. The weather was perfect so we held the action on the poop deck at the stern. A stage was set up, seating organised and all the passengers attended, some claiming their seats an hour in advance of the show. Those who didn't have seating had plenty of vantage points to stand and observe all the action. I had a cameo part in the proceedings, which was recorded and shown on film, welcoming Mr Hope and his party on board the *Liberte*. It was interesting to observe that when Mr Hope was performing his famous monologue, an assistant would hold up huge sheets of cardboard with prompts written on them in large letters so that Mr Hope gave a performance as if he were doing it all from memory. That was an art in itself.

With Jonathan Winters.

From left to right, Sports Director Sarah Foreman, Howard Keel & Barbara Beck, Tahiti manager of land operations.

Barbara Biondi, Chief Purser, with Jonathan Winters.

After filming, Mr Hope and his party, together with some officers, retired to the "Le Club" for an aperitif before the evening meal. I managed to circulate between all the guests and had some very interesting conversations.

In Conversation with John Denver & partner.

Mr Hope, his wife Delores and Jonathan Winters were seated at my table for the evening meal. As the conversation flowed, I remarked to Mr Hope that he looked fit and healthy, and asked if he had any medical problems. He replied, "When I was 76 I began to have memory problems: when I went to a public toilet and came out, I realised I hadn't zipped up my fly. Now I'm 83, my memory problems have got worse: when I go to a public toilet, I forget to zip down."

There was a lull in the conversation, when a telephone sounded, *buz-buz buz-buz*. I really thought it was a real telephone, but it was Jonathan Winters imitating the noise. Mr Winters lifted up an imaginary telephone and said, "Hello," and in a completely different voice he started holding a two-way conversation with himself, asking questions and answering them in two different tones of voice. It was an amazing act and so funny, in fact, I thought that Mr Winters was more humorous than Mr Hope.

Bob Hope, wife Delores and the Everhard family at the Captain's Table.

After dinner about 10 p.m. I escorted the party ashore via our tender to their hotel. We said our farewells and I returned to the ship.

In February 1987 I received orders to proceed to San Francisco for drydocking and had no idea what was to follow. When we arrived in San Francisco and went into drydock I was informed that the *Liberte* was going to be sold and to make inventories of all equipment and a record of all cabin keys. This was another exhaustive exercise and took a couple of weeks. The inventory and documents were handed over to an American Hawaii Cruises representative. The Officers, including myself and Crew were given a month's salary and repatriated to their country of origin. So ended a beautiful Tahitian experience.

Chapter Eight

Life After Polynesia

AFTER LEAVING THE LIBERTE and returning home, I took life easy for a couple of months. I was 55 years old and some people retire at that age but I sent out a few C.V.'s to various passenger ship companies without much success but eventually did receive a reply to go for an interview with Ocean Cruise Line of London, the company David Lynn had joined. I suspect he had recommended me when my C.V. had arrived at their offices. I duly went down to London for an interview with the owner, arriving in the morning, but the owner was delayed and my interview was postponed until the afternoon. That proved to have disastrous consequences for me. I went for lunch at a local Indian restaurant for a highly spiced curry and pint of beer. Don't ever emulate that example if you are going for a job interview! When I did attend the interview later in the afternoon, I must have smelt like an Indian restaurant come brewery. Needless to say, I didn't have a successful interview.

The next job hunting experience I had was with a Greek company who were building a couple of luxury yachts, carrying about 80 passengers and scheduled to sail around the Mediterranean. I had to go to Athens for an interview for the position as superintendent and relief Captain. The interview was successful, my monthly salary agreed and I spent a few days studying the yacht plans, making a few alteration recommendations and investigating the facilities and amenities of the proposed ports of call. After a while, I told the owner that as the yachts were only in the early stage of building and they had a consultant attending the building, I could continue performing my work at home, which would save the costs of hotel accommodation and meals for me, to which he readily agreed.

After a few weeks at home involved with making a list and costs of charts which would be required to cover the area intended to cruise, compiling a company rules handbook and many other detailed items, I discovered that my monthly salary and expenses had not been credited into my bank account. I had been in regular telephone contact with the company and the telephone bill was quite high. Alarm bells started to ring and I phoned the company to complain that my salary and expenses had not been credited to my bank account. They assured me there must be some mistake and they would investigate. The next time I rang them I couldn't get through and so it remained until I wrote to the Airline and Seafarer Officers union explaining my predicament and approximate monies owing me. They sent a letter to the Greek company and the monies involved were deposited into my bank account post haste. That's the last contact I had with that company.

Soon after the Greek experience, I received a phone call from my friend Adrian Chapmen, who had been Chief Engineer on the Caribbean Progress when we had the engine room fire. He was now employed as a Lloyds surveyor in the Persian Gulf Ports. He asked me if I would help a ship owner friend of his out by going as relief captain on a small cargo ship trading in and around the Gulf. I was at a loose end so agreed, joining the *Socotra*, an old 1,600 ton cargo vessel in Dubai. The captain and crew were Pakistani and the captain claimed he was taking three months leave because he wanted to be with his children during the school holidays. It also happened to coincide with the beginning of the monsoon season which lasts three months, when the weather is continuously bad, strong winds, torrential rain and very rough seas.

The three months experience was interesting, with continuous bad weather and numerous incidents. On one occasion, proceeding to Aden to discharge our cargo of cement with rough seas on our port beam, the cargo shifted and we developed quite a large starboard list. With the possibility of capsizing, I successfully manoeuvred and ballasted the ship to reduce the listing, so preventing the catastrophe. During this period, until the situation became stable, some of the crew, who were visibly frightened and I'm sure were praying, congregated on the navigation bridge. On arrival in Aden I was fined by the Harbour Master for being overloaded due to the ballasting. The reason for being overloaded, my actions to avert a catastrophe, were not accepted as extenuating circumstances. After all the hassle, the Harbour

Master had the gall to ask me for a couple of bottles of spirits and some cigarettes. Of course, I politely refused.

After my three months relief period, the monsoon season had come to an end, the weather returned to normal with light winds, smooth seas, the Pakistani Captain returned to the ship and I returned home. About a couple of weeks later, the owner of the company contacted me and offered me the marine superintendent and relief captain's position, but after my previous experiences I knew I would be relief captain for the monsoon seasons and superintendent in the "off" season, so I declined.

As both Jacqui and I enjoyed being in Florida, I decided to take a six month holiday in Florida every year from November to April to escape the English winter while we were both in reasonable health, because at some stage in our lives we might not be physically able to travel, which proved the case. We rented a condominium located in Clearwater from Sylvia Ventimeglia, who had been Purser on the *Veracruz* and was still following her seagoing career, so the condo was empty. We spent quite a good deal of our time, including Christmas celebrations, with our friends Ann and Aka Suliaman who lived nearby. I helped Aka to convert his double garage into two apartments which they rented out. One of the apartments was rented by an American couple, Jim and Sharon, who had a restaurant which they said hadn't been successful due to the location it was in. They were looking to undertake another restaurant venture in a better location.

Ann & Aka Suliaman.

One day they said they had found the ideal spot in Tarpon Springs, whose population is predominately Greek/American on the West Coast of Florida, about 20 miles from Clearwater and actually in a yacht basin and invited Ann and Aka to see it. Jacqui and I tagged along. It had previously been a bar/games room/restaurant and seated 150. The location appeared ideal, plenty of parking facilities, with a wooden deck at the rear of the restaurant and extended pier leading into the yacht basin. They couldn't finance the project by themselves, so invited Ann and Aka, Jacqui and I to become partners in the venture. It seemed a good idea at the time so we agreed. I became a silent partner because I didn't have a "green card" which would have enabled me to have business dealings in the U.S.A. Ann and Aka were naturalised American subjects so were able to be involved in all business dealings. We divided the funding three ways: I provided the cash for my share of the business, Ann and Aka provided their share but Jim and Sharon claimed their money was tied up elsewhere but they would be getting it in a couple of weeks, so I provided their share on the understanding that they would repay me in one month's time. It seemed plausible that Jim and Sharon should sign the lease agreement with the owner of the building, as they had experience running a restaurant, and were American citizens, so they were able to apply for a license to operate a restaurant. As partners we signed a separate agreement regarding the funding and running of the place.

The deal was done and we set about redecorating and building a Tahitian type bar on the outside decking. We named the restaurant "The Jolly Crab" and planned to specialize in seafood. Fishing boats landed their catch of fish, shrimp and crabs nearby, so we were able to obtain and serve really fresh seafood.

Outside Tahitian Bar.

After a month, with all the redecorating completed, we were able to have the Public Health Inspectors attend to see if we complied with the Health Regulations. We passed with flying colours and were issued our license.

Inside Restaurant with seascape mural.

Our head chef was one of the American partners, Jim, whose speciality was large scrumptious fish cakes with his own special seasoning. His wife Sharon was in charge of the bar, Aka was in charge of the accounts and I was a general dogsbody. We also employed two other people as waitresses and an assistant chef.

One of the Manila Connection, Rolly Rodriguez, had married Cindy, one of the American Cashiers he had met on the *Veracruz*. Rolly had given up his sea life and I believe was working at that time in the Tampa Airport. I contacted and arranged with him to provide live music at the "Jolly Crab" on a Saturday and Sunday evening. Rolly proved to be very popular and the live music attracted many customers.

Sharon gave me a cheque for the money I had advanced to them at the beginning of the venture but the cheque bounced. She claimed there had been some mistake and it was rectified later but I should have taken heed of the warnings that were ringing in my head.

After the six months in Florida, with our American visa time running out, the restaurant seemingly going well as an excellent business and becoming well established, Jacqui and I returned home for the summer.

When we returned again in the autumn for our scheduled six-month holiday, Jim and Sharon had taken over the accounting of the restaurant's finances and did not want Aka involved in the business in any way. They claimed the business was not doing well and the atmosphere between us became very strained. After a while I could see that it would be in my best interest to sell my portion of the business to Jim and Sharon. They claimed they did not have the finances to buy me out but would pay 200 dollars per month into my bank account until my portion in the venture had been paid back. I drew up an agreement which was witnessed and signed, then withdrew from any involvement in the Restaurant.

After the six months in Florida, we again returned home. No monies were being credited in my bank account and when I tried to contact Sharon by telephone I could never get through. After a while the telephone seemed to have been disconnected.

When we returned to Florida for our winter holidays, it seemed as if Jim and Sharon had done a "moonlight flit" from the Restaurant and also from the apartment they rented from Ann and Aka, leaving debts and I imagine wages due to the employees. I was told that they had a "going away, moonlight flit party" at the Restaurant, loading most of the equipment and stock into a lorry. I could not find out where they had "flitted" to and didn't have the inclination to find them in any case, because recovering my cash would have cost more than what they owed me. I just put it down to a bad experience but I know, even if they don't, that one day they will be judged by the ultimate judge.

During our second winter visit to Florida, Jacqui and I came to the decision that we should move permanently to Florida. A house building project called Brigadoon, located in a park, surrounding a lake was being developed in Tampa. We went viewing and put a deposit on a house. The house was a three-story town house, the master bedroom being on the ground floor with French windows opening onto a grassed section leading down to the lake. It was a beautiful location, all kinds of wild-life, with notices to beware of crocodiles. When we returned home we put our house on the market and after only two weeks we had a buyer. However, before the sale was signed, sealed and delivered, I had second thoughts and changed my mind about moving to Florida. It was fortunate that I did, because after a couple of years, Jacqui developed Multiple Sclerosis and the medical bills in the U.S.A. would have bankrupted us. My deposit on the house in Florida was returned.

Our last visit to Florida was in December 1997. Two days after arriving, Jacqui tripped over a curb and broke a bone in her foot. We went to the local hospital and the receptionist asked if we had insurance to pay for the hospital bills, which of course we had and everyone travelling overseas should not be without. We had over an hour to wait for treatment until the receptionist had contacted the company with whom we had taken the insurance out with. Apparently, she was being passed from one department to another until she at last got confirmation that the insurance company would cover the medical costs. Once the confirmation had been received, treatment progressed rapidly, with blood tests, several ex-rays from different directions of the foot and finally a special boot fitted. Jacqui was required to attend the hospital every two weeks for a progress examination and further ex-rays from all directions. Four weeks later we were on our way home. About a month after arriving home, we received the copy of an interim bill sent to the insurance company which was itemised and amounted to over three thousand dollars. I don't know what the final account was because we didn't receive any further copies.

In 1989 I was approached by Captain Malcolm Whitely, who was one of the Elder Brethren of Hull Trinity House and he, as my sponsor, invited me to apply to join the Guild or Brotherhood of Masters and Pilots, Seamen of the Hull Trinity House. This involved submitting records to prove that I was qualified and had been in command of ships for at least three years, references from past employers, also that both parents were British Subjects when I was born. When those conditions were met, I was required to undertake a pilotage examination by the 18-member board for the areas Hull, Northward to Scotland, Hull, Eastward to Germany and Hull, Southward to the Downs. It is a very precise examination, requiring knowledge of the courses involved, description of dangers, lighthouses and buoys encountered. The pilotage examination is known as the lesson and is contained in nine closely typed pages of information. The only condition I did not meet was that when I was born, my father was a Norwegian subject and it required a special dispensation from the board of Trinity House to proceed with the examination, which I passed on the 25th of April 1990 and so became a member of the Guild of Masters and Pilots, Seamen of Hull Trinity House.

The city of Kingston upon Hull has a Triple Crown logo and one of the jewels in that logo is the Trinity House, a beautiful building, rebuilt in 1753 and containing many artefacts, mainly of a marine nature. Stepping over the threshold into the building is like stepping into a different world. The history and artefacts contained in the "house" is recorded in three volumes of books written by Captain Arthur Storey, deceased, a former Elder Brother and Master Warden of Trinity House. Additional interesting information written by Professor Donald Woodward, Archivist of Trinity House, is contained in his booklet, *The Trinity House of Kingston upon Hull*. Professor Woodward also published a booklet entitled *Trafalgar; 21 October 1805, A Hull Man's Account of the Battle*. It is about a man called Abraham Turner, an ex-Trinity House Schoolboy, who was the master's mate on the *H.M.S. Africa* during the Battle of Trafalgar. He reported an account of the battle in a letter to the Brethren of Trinity House.

Hull Trinity House is not open to the general public, except by organised groups of not more than 12 people who have previously applied to the Secretary for a tour. Inside "The House" the various rooms and passageways are kept in pristine condition by a dedicated squad of ladies who second as very efficient wine waitresses at numerous functions throughout the year, culminating in a very impressive Christmas Luncheon, which is attended by the Trustees, Honorary Brethren and Civic Dignitaries.

The Courtroom.

The Council Room, still strewn with rushes in the medieval manner.

With all its awe-inspiring artefacts full of history, it is also a working building where 18 members of the Board of Trustees of the guild meet at least three days of the week to carry out their business and monitoring of the Corporate and self funding Charity responsibilities.

There are six committees. The Pilotage committee, who examine Captains that have applied for their North Sea Pilots Licence and also for the renewal of that licence. They also liaise with London and Newcastle Trinity House concerning pilotage matters.

The Buildings committee is involved with the operation and upkeep of several farms, shops and sanctioning any repair requirements. The Finance committee sanctions any financial requests. The Audit committee audits any transactions they may think appropriate. The Conservation committee keep a record of all the artefacts, examine for condition and sight any additional artefact gifts that may have been donated. The Grants committee mainly oversees the running of the Rest Homes and sanction any requests for pensions if the applicant meets the various rules and requirements of the charity. The Rest Homes, 58 high quality flats and eight bungalows, including a recreation building, are set in their own well-tended grounds. My mum and dad spent the sunset years of their lives happily occupying flat 58 at the Rest Homes. Over 800 people with marine connections receive a quarterly grant.

There are 18 members on the board of Hull Trinity House Trustees, 12 Elder Brethren and 6 assistants, the number being set by the Royal Charter of Elizabeth the First in 1581. Two of the Elder Brethren are elected annually as Master Warden (Chairman) serving for a period of six months each. Each successive monarch issues Royal Charters mainly confirming the conditions contained in the previous Charter. These Charters are suitably displayed in a secure room. In 2009 there were nine Trinity House School old boys and Captain Thompson, a former Headmaster of the school on the board. There is a wealth of experience and knowledge amongst the 18 trustees who are aware of the high standards by previous board members they have to maintain and pass on to future members.

There are also 4 Honorary Brethren, His Royal Highness Prince Philip, Prince Charles, Mr. Andrew Marr, a well known Kingston upon Hull trawler owner and Lt. General Sir Michael Gray, K.C.B., O.B.E., D.L., a retired

Paratrooper Regiment Officer. The Duke of Edinburgh, Prince Philip, attends the Hull Trinity House Christmas Luncheon about every three years.

Election to the board is by a vote of all the guild members, which occurs whenever there is a death, retirement through ill health or resignation. I was elected to the board in 1998 and resigned in January 2010 to care full time for my wife Jacqui, whose M.S. had progressed to such a degree that she has chronic mobility problems.

During the time I was a member of the board; I served on all the committees and was elected Master Warden in 2006 to 2007.

On being elected to the board as a trustee, you are also elected to serve as a founder governor of the Hull Trinity House School. There are eight members of the board who are founder governors and as a new member is elected to the board the senior founder school governor resigns so that there are always eight members of the board involved directly with the school. The chairman of governors is always a member of the board.

I was a school governor for ten years, from 1998 to 2008, serving on the Headmaster's Assessment and Disciplinary Committees, also being link governor for religious education and special needs.

There is a vast difference between how the school operated in my schooldays and now. In my time, about 95 per cent of the boys chose a successful seagoing career, either in the Merchant Navy, Royal Navy, Pilotage Service or Fishing Service. Now only about one per cent chooses a seagoing career. Also, there were only 130 students, whereas now there are 290, which is small compared to other schools, but small is perfect, or nearly so. Unfortunately, the modern trend by successive governments to make schools financially viable is to make them as large as possible, from 600 pupils upwards and I think through being large the individual link between teacher and pupil is lost.

In gratitude for the start in the nautical career the school gave me, I donated an annual Religious Education Prize which will go on for perpetuity. It is presented in July on prize day, along with a host of other prizes to the pupil showing the most aptitude and dedication in that subject. I always receive a letter of thanks from the boy receiving the R.E. prize, which, for me, is very gratifying.

The school has a dedicated Headmaster, Staff, board of Governors and consistently tops the annual attainment league of secondary schools in the jurisdiction of the Local Education Authority of Kingston upon Hull. Mr. Twaits, the Headmaster, is continually exploring and supporting new ideas and innovations to improve the already high standards achieved by the "Trinity" school. The school has a ceremonial naval uniform which is worn by senior pupils, known as "The White Squad" because the trousers are white linen material. The "White Squad" are often requested to form a guard of honour on civic occasions and also when there is a visit to the town by Royalty. In my schooldays, all the pupils wore the uniform with white duck canvas trousers, which were much stiffer and uncomfortable, compared to the modern day "whites".

White squad being inspected by The Queen & Prince Philip, accompanied by Susan Cunliffe-Lister, Lord Lieutenant of the East Riding of Yorkshire.

One innovation which has been in action for several years at the school is the Pupils Support Unit or P.S.U., headed by Mrs Paulette Waterman. This is where pupils who have been excluded temporarily from a lesson for some misdemeanour or disruption in the classroom are sent to continue their studies under strict supervision. Mrs Waterman is also the person who contacts the "bad" boy's parents to relate the misdemeanour and if warranted, after consultation with the Headmaster, Mr Twaits, to request them to collect the boy from the school for a period of exclusion.

As link governor with matters of discipline, I often visited the unit and had heart to heart talks with any boys there, which wasn't very often. The "house" is adjacent to the school, separated only by the chapel, so it is very convenient for the Brethren who are governors to visit the school and keep in close contact with events.

Captain Stuart Ledger, an Elder Brethren and I gave "mock" job interviews on request to year eleven students. Captain Ledger had a unique gift of giving advice on what questions would be asked, body language to adopt and the answers to give at an interview. I gave advice on what not to do (eat a curry and have a pint before the interview). The success rate when Students had taken the "mock" interview and attended the real thing was a hundred per cent. Some boys, who attended more than one interview, were successful and spoilt for choice.

During term time, the first Monday in the month, I conducted an Assembly with year seven pupils and still do, even though I have resigned my position as School Governor. I have different subjects at each Assembly but always include a special verse from the book of 1 Samuel chapter 16 verse 7 which states:

> "But the Lord said to Samuel, Do not consider his appearance or his height, for I have rejected him. The Lord does not look at the things man looks at. Man looks at the outward appearance, but the Lord looks at the heart."

I have a quiz and the prizes are varied but duplicated. Into one of the prizes I secrete a £5 note to illustrate the lesson that although outwardly the prize may appear the same as another, it isn't always the case and you cannot judge by outward appearances. Most times I get to keep my £5 note and the quiz participants are disappointed with only a prize but sometimes the lucky ones get their reward. There is always plenty of advice from the onlookers which prize to select.

I enjoyed the time I was a school governor but I don't know how schools can recruit teachers and governors now, especially since regulations and the curriculum are being changed more often than the Minister for Education in the past few years. It seems as if successive Ministers of Education are not really interested in Education, only interested in bringing their name to the attention of the public for political gains, sadly, to the detriment of the educational system.

Chapter Nine

Born Again

IN 1993 when we were taking our winter break in Florida and at a loose end on a Sunday, our friends Ann and Aka Suliaman who were Christians and attended the Clearwater Calvary Baptist Church, invited Jacqui and I to go along with them. When we were children, both Jacqui and I had been in church choirs; as adults we attended a Church of England church occasionally as most people do, for Weddings, Baptisms and Funerals.

I have never attended a church anything like the Clearwater Calvary Baptist Church then or since. The main church building was huge, with small television screens scattered around the various sections towards the back, so people could see what was going on. Other buildings and offices radiated from and were adjacent to the main church. The Pastor was Bill Anderson, Associate Pastor Ray Jones, with Ministers of Music, Administration, Education, Youth, Children, Adults, Evangelism and numerous other Ministers. Six lady secretaries were shared between the various departments. There were two services on a Sunday morning to accommodate the congregation which numbered at least 2,000 members each time and also one service on a Sunday night. An orchestra of about 20 provided the music and choir with about 120 members leading the hymn singing. At the end of the service, the Pastor invited everyone to remain seated, bow their heads and close their eyes; anyone who felt the Spirit moving them could make their way to the front of the church where attendants would be waiting to hear and witness their declaration that Jesus was Lord. We really enjoyed the church experience but did not initially make a commitment to become "Born again Christians".

Calvary Baptist Church.

We had attended the Church on three or four occasions and on the forth occasion, when we were leaving the church, Jacqui said, "Someone is calling my name." I looked around and there were several people about. "Someone must be talking to a person called Jacqui," I replied. The following Sunday we were delayed leaving and Jacqui said, "Someone's calling my name again!" I looked around and there was no-one in the vicinity. The following Sunday, December the 5th 1993, after the Pastor made his invitation, I opened my eyes and Jacqui had gone to the front of the church to acknowledge that Jesus Christ was her Lord and Saviour.

We also attended, with about 300 other people, a Wednesday night bible study conducted by Pastor Anderson. On Wednesday the 9th February 1994, after the bible study class, which was about the Holy Trinity, we were on our way out and I remarked to Jacqui that I didn't understand how the Holy Trinity could be three in one. She said, "Why not ask Pastor Anderson?" He was surrounded by a group of people wanting his attention, so I remarked that he was too busy. As I was still looking, the group parted as if by magic and Pastor Anderson came walking towards me. I stopped him and told him that I didn't understand how God could be three in one. He remarked that not many people do understand but if I considered water in three forms, the original form, steam, and ice, they were all from the same source, water, just as the Holy Trinity is from the same source, God. Then he said, "Anderson, isn't it time you accepted Jesus Christ as your Lord and Saviour?" I had my arms folded and they unfolded on their own accord and dropped to my side. I heard a voice saying, "Yes"—which I realised was mine and I repeated the sinner's pray and I acknowledged that Jesus Christ was my Lord and Saviour. By making that statement I became a Born Again Christian.

The Baptistery was at the front of the church, about 30 feet above the choir. It was a large glass-fronted unit, filled with warm water with about four steps leading into the Baptistery, a section of flat flooring and then about four steps leading out of the unit. Sound microphones and T.V. cameras were fitted so that the entire congregation was involved and able to witness the baptisms.

On Sunday January 16th 1994, Jacqui with several other people were baptized by Pastor Bill Anderson by total immersion in water before the second morning service. Baptists are baptized by total immersion to symbolize the believer's death to sin before they are submerged in the water and their resurrection to new life in Christ when they emerge from the water. Before immersion, Pastor Bill asks, "What have you to declare" and the answer given is, "Jesus is Lord." Some people believe that baptism by total immersion is when they become Born Again Christians but I believe it is when they first accept that Jesus is Lord. I was baptized in March 1994.

We became involved with church activities, joining a sign language class but that only lasted a few lessons because Jacqui was finding it difficult due to her arthritis.

There was an appeal at a Sunday morning service by John and Brenda Grampsas who ran a children's programme on a Saturday morning called "Kid's World" for volunteers to help with the programme. This involved attending the children's programme on a Saturday morning and making visits around the housing projects on a Thursday at 4 p.m. after school, to talk to the children and parents and issue a few "goodies". On a Saturday morning, Jacqui was assigned to be a greeter when the children arrived for "Kids World" and I was assigned to be a bus captain which was a bit different to being a sea captain. Seven buses went out to the various areas picking up about 300 children and someone had to ride with each bus to try and keep order. Being British, speaking differently and also having a few tricks up my sleeve, I managed to keep order on my bus pretty well. When the very small children got to know Jacqui, they would alight from the bus and run to her to be picked up and swung around. The bigger children would just come to her for a hug.

Buses lined up to leave Kid's World.

Arriving at the church buildings for the Saturday Sunday school, the children dispersed to the various rooms according to age group. Jacqui and I were assigned to be involved with children aged 9 to 12. Every week there was a different verse from the bible displayed at the front of the room. At the beginning of the session, children were asked if anyone remembered the previous week's verse and rewards given for those who remembered. Children were given a bible as a prize for whoever could recite all the books of the bible in order.

I became involved with learning to operate hand puppets, which was a good training opportunity because when we returned home I started a church puppet group and had plenty of volunteers from the children to learn the intricacies of manipulating a hand puppet.

When we returned home from our six-month vacation in Florida in 1994, we started looking around for a Baptist Church to attend. Consulting the telephone directory, we couldn't find the telephone number or address of any

Churches, but we did find the telephone number of Gideons International. Phoning the Gideons, we spoke to Mr Ken Gibbs who informed us that he and his wife Grace attended the Boulevard Baptist Church on a Sunday night and arranged to meet us there. The Boulevard was near Bean Street so I was quite familiar with the area. The church members were very friendly and welcomed us with open arms and after attending for a couple of months we became members. The Pastor was Michael Hawden. He was married to Doreen and had two boys, Gareth and Martin. Later, looking in the telephone directory, the numbers and addresses of churches were there… God moves in mysterious ways!

Towards the end of 1994, before we took our six-month vacation period in Florida, Doreen, our Pastor Michael's wife, died. I had an insurance policy set to mature and had plans to change our car for a newer model. I scanned the local paper for any bargains, made phone calls and arrangements with a company to go for a test drive. That night I had a dream, and a voice said, *do not buy a car—give Michael one thousand pounds to take himself and his boys on holiday*. In the morning I told Jacqui about the dream. Ignoring the instructions, I went ahead and bought the car. It was the worst car I have ever possessed and eventually changed it eight months later.

We went out to Florida on the 15th November 1994 for our usual winter break, and received a lovely welcome from our friends and the children in "Kid's World", and we picked up our church activities as if we hadn't been away.

The statistics for 1995 were: total attendance of children aged 4 to 13 year olds and upwards in 45 weeks 16,909, averaging 376, with the largest attendance of 688. During the year, bus crews kept a lookout for families who were in need of help. Their names and addresses were recorded and assistance was given by a Calvary Church programme called "Life Line". Just before Thanksgiving on the 24th November 1994, volunteers including Jacqui and I, prepared Thanksgiving shopping certificates to be issued to the people recorded as in need. The shopping certificates were to the value of fifteen dollars or ten pounds in English money, enough to buy a good sized turkey with money left over. We delivered the certificates to the named person on the Thursday visiting day. The joy and thankfulness of the reciprocates was overwhelming at times. One lady we gave an envelope to, opened it, screamed and ran around with delight!

At Christmas time the church erected a large Christmas tree in the foyer of the church with labels attached to the branches containing the names of the children, their shoe and dress or shirt sizes. Members of the congregation were invited to either make a donation or provide clothing and presents for each child. It was quite a mammoth task for the volunteers' co-coordinating the presents with the children, then wrapping them up in Christmas wrapping paper. 450 parcels were loaded onto the seven buses by volunteers about one week prior to Christmas and distributed to the parents of the children, to be opened on Christmas Day amid much excitement from the reciprocates.

On Boxing Day 1994, we received a telephone call from our Pastor in England, Michael Hawden, saying he had received a certain amount of cash from the Yorkshire Baptist Association telling him to take his two boys on a holiday. He didn't know where to take them but had been advised by one of the church members to give us a call and see if we could show them around Florida. Of course we agreed and I told him that he could stay with us and we would arrange to take him and the boys to Disney World in Orlando. I took care of the arrangements, booking accommodation in a Motel and a three-day pass to the Disney World attractions, also visiting Sea World and Bushe Gardens. Michael and the boys arrived in Florida on the 1st of January 1995 and departed on the 12th. During that time, besides touring the attractions, Michael became involved with Kids World and was presented to the Clearwater Calvary Church congregation by Pastor Anderson and he gave a talk about the Boulevard Baptist Church. I paid the expenses for us all, including tours, accommodation, etc., by credit card, and it amounted to about £1,000. As I said before, God moves in mysterious ways, His wonders to perform. His will is done one way or another.

Michael was so impressed with the Kids World programme that when he returned to Hull, with the help of church members, he started an after school club in partnership with Youth for Christ, involving Primary Schoolchildren, aged 7 to 11 year olds, called "Zone 3", which averaged 36 members.

About the 4th Of December 1994 a friend of Jacqui's called Lyn Jones mentioned during bible class that she had met a couple of ladies, Irene and Kindra, who were "looking for something" but couldn't find it no matter which church they went to. Lyn witnessed to them and suggested they come to Calvary Baptist Church with her. All the church members were asked to pray for them during the service. Jacqui said that she prayed and prayed that their hearts would be touched by Jesus to receive the precious gift of God's Salvation. At the altar call they went forward to acknowledge Jesus is Lord. Jacqui said that she had become elated and felt a happiness she had not felt before. After the service, Jacqui went to welcome them into the family of God. Being propelled forward towards them a path seemed to open up as the congregation had started leaving the church going in the opposite direction. Jacqui's eyes shone and her face was radiant with an iridescent glow. I noticed it, and so did Lyn, the two ladies, and a host of other people. Lyn phoned Jacqui the following day and told her that Irene and Kindra couldn't get over the radiance of Jacqui's face, mentioning it over and over again. Both ladies were baptized on Christmas day 1994. During the week 18th to 25th December 1994, the estranged husband of one of the ladies made contact with her and renewed married life. Lyn remarked that "Jesus even repairs marriages". Early in January the husband became Born Again and was later baptized.

On the 11th January 1995, Pastor Ray Jones asked us to make a visit to two families with English connections. The first family consisted of dad Andrew, mum Tausha and three children. The mum was a Christian but not the English dad, Andrew. We visited and fellowshipped. Andrew was in the process of laying a new carpet so I gave him a hand to lay it and we talked about life in England compared to life in the States. On our second visit Tausha asked Jacqui to give her testimony. We became good friends and the two older children attended the church's children's weekly AWANA programme. One year later Andrew and the two older children became Born Again Christians and were baptized. Tausha renewing her commitment to the Lord.

The second visit was to a family consisting of mum, Debra, who was English and three lovely children, Marlaina, Austin and Alexandra. Debra was very depressed and had phoned for help. She was curled up in the corner of a settee and appeared to have no interest in anything. There didn't appear to be any food in the house so Marlaina escorted us to the local supermarket where we bought a box full of essential food items for them. After this initial visit we went two or three times a week and formed a very good bonding with the family. Debra was a very intelligent, gifted person; she could play the piano like a concert pianist, and the violin, and had been part of the Calvary Baptist Church orchestra. We started picking the children up from school and taking them to the various children's programmes and church on a Sunday. With our support, encouragement and involvement with the children, Debra slowly came out of her depressed state and took a course in nursing, which she completed and qualified as a nurse.

On Saturday April 15ᵗʰ 1995 at Kids World a young girl came up to Jacqui and asked, "Are you the lady that takes Marlaina to church?" Jacqui confirmed that she was. "Can I come to church with you tomorrow?" she asked. Jacqui told her that she could but needed her parents' permission. The young girl was called Amanda and when we took Marlaina and Austin home we also gave Amanda a lift because she lived quite near Marlaina. Amanda introduced us to her parents who readily gave their permission for us to collect Amanda and take her to church. On Sunday evening we picked up both girls and during the church service Amanda whispered to Jacqui, "I want to ask Jesus into my heart." At the end of the service both Amanda and Marlaina went forward at the altar call and both prayed the prayer of salvation.

On April 23ʳᵈ 1995 Marlaina was baptized by total immersion. Amanda was baptized after we left Florida on April the 30ᵗʰ. Her parents wanted the whole family present. It transpired that Amanda's grandfather and another member of the family had been baptized some years earlier at the Calvary Baptist Church and the family was coming to witness the baptism from all over the U.S.A.

April 23ʳᵈ 1995: Marlaina being baptized by total immersion.

On April 27th 1995 we returned home and became involved in the Zone 3 children's programme and I organised The Boulevard Baptist Church Puppet Group. My granddaughter Kaylee and her friend Sophie were the mainstay of the group but all the children were interested and the best manipulators of the puppets constituted the group. I built a special stage which the children operated behind so that only the puppets were in view. Pastor Michael had a great sense of humour and together we composed some outstanding biblical scripts for the puppet plays. We would record the plays on tape; then the children would practice to co-ordinate the operation of the puppets' mouths with the words coming from the tape, so that it appeared as if the puppets were speaking. Our granddaughter Kaylee was 6-years-old when she started learning to manipulate the puppets and became quite an expert. She continued until she was about 18, when boys became her main interest as is usual for teenaged girls! The group performed at churches and clubs all over the Yorkshire area, as well as special events at public places in Kingston upon Hull. Kaylee was also my assistant when I performed my "magic with a meaning" at these public places.

In Queens Gardens, Hull City Centre. Puppeteers Stuart Higginbotham, Granddaughter Kaylee (manipulating two puppets), Elizabeth Walker.

Proceeding to allocated pitch in Hull City Centre with assistant
Granddaughter Kaylee carrying the box of tricks.

In July 1995 we received a letter from John and Brenda Grampsas of Kids World, Clearwater Calvary Baptist Church, inviting us to accompany them on a six-day visit to Brooklyn, New York and experience the Metro Ministries children's programme and training sessions run by Pastor Bill Wilson. Bill Wilson is renowned all over the U.S.A. for his children's programme; in fact, he has expanded and established the format of his programmes in Canada, the U.K., Holland, Germany, Malaysia, Sweden, Switzerland, Taiwan, Haiti, South Africa, the Philippines, India and Romania. He has also written books and made videos.

The visit was to start on Wednesday September the 27th and last until Monday the 2nd of October. We had not scheduled any visit to the States before November and we did not have the finances to make the extra trip, but to experience Metro Ministries in New York was seemingly an opportunity too good to miss. Jacqui and I prayed about it because it involved flying to Florida, then New York, back to Florida and then home. We made enquiries about flights, prices and prayed some more.

Out of the blue, a letter came for Jacqui from the Inland Revenue containing a cheque to the value of £653, which was for repayment of tax overcharged for 1985. The next day *another* letter arrived from the Inland Revenue containing a cheque to the value of £653 for Jacqui. Jacqui thought the Inland Revenue had made a mistake and wanted to return the second cheque. I had a look at the letter and it was for repayment of tax overcharged for 1986. *£653 was the exact airfare for one ticket U.K./Florida/New York/Florida/U.K.* God moves in mysterious ways, His wonders to perform!

We flew to Tampa, Florida on September 12th and on to New York on September 27th. The Metro Ministries were located in old large brewery buildings, in a district of Brooklyn called Bushwick. There was a wayside pulpit notice on the side of the building making a statement from the bible in the book of Proverbs, chapter 22, verse 6: "Train a child the way he should go, and when he is old he will not turn from it." The Sunday school was on a Saturday morning and afternoon 10 a.m. and 1 p.m. 45 buses transported about 1,000 children each time from the neighbourhood and back home. In the afternoon at 3 p.m. there was a programme called the "Kangaroo Class" for children aged 3 to 6 year olds with special needs, some being born with drug problems inherited from their mums at birth.

During the week on schooldays, nine trucks went out into local school areas and had a programme called Sidewalk Sunday School, Christian based with songs, fun and games. The trucks had been modified so that one side of the truck came down revealing a stage from which the Metro Ministry personnel would conduct the singing, games and activities. A large tarpaulin was laid on the ground adjacent to the truck and about 60 children would congregate with parents watching on. 27 Metro Ministries staff were involved in this programme covering 27 of the toughest neighbourhood sites in New York. Jacqui accompanied one of the sidewalk Sunday schools, taking a minor part in the presentation of the programme. She also visited a school and distributed leaflets on the streets.

Since 1995 the New York Metro Ministries have expanded to new buildings, more staff, more buses, more sites and ministers to thousands more children in that area.

One of the staff, Cheryl, who seconded as a bus driver, was assigned to take me under her wing and I accompanied her, collecting the children and taking them back home on a Saturday. My English (Hull) accent and "magic" worked wonders again and I became quite popular with the kids.

Midweek, I accompanied Cheryl in predominately black crime ridden areas, visiting the homes of the children who attended the Metro Ministries programme. We travelled by the Metro Ministries bus with a group of local children who were our "minders". At one block of flats, the elevator was not working, the lights were out and several unsavoury characters were hanging around the entrance, which smelt strongly of stale urine. Cheryl had previously warned me not to make eye contact, to just carry on if spoken to and stick near the kids. The kids kind of surrounded us and obviously knew the characters because one of them said, "Hi Joe, these people are from the Metro Ministries and we're just visiting." "Hi," Joe replied, showing just a mild interest and giving us a cursory look. We did not make eye contact and just started climbing the very dirty stairs up to the eighth floor. When we reached the apartment, Cheryl knocked on the door and shouted, "Hi, it's Cheryl, come to visit." Locks and bolts were opened as if it was Fort Knox and we entered, with all the kids, into a room containing about five more kids and a mum. The children ran to Cheryl and hugged her as if their lives depended on it. With all of us in the room, it was standing room only. Cheryl distributed some "goodies" to the children and introduced me to the mum. Her children told her I was the "magic" man and I had to do a demonstration. Fortunately, I had brought a couple of my stock tricks with me so my reputation as the "magic" man stayed intact.

The visiting carried on in much the same fashion for the rest of the time, which took about two hours. It was quite scary and I was pleased and relieved when the visiting period was completed without any incident. Cheryl and her co-workers are very committed going into these areas the way they do. Before the buses go out there is a prayer meeting for a successful and safe visitation and I'm sure plenty of silent individual prayers were said during the visitations.

On the way back to base, to show my appreciation to the kids for their "minders" duties, I asked Cheryl to stop at a MacDonalds and I invited them all to a "Big Mac" and can of coke, which appeared to be the highlight of their day.

All too soon this uplifting experience came to an end and it was time to return to Florida.

During the time we were in Bushwick, Jacqui and I had a 45-minute meeting with the Pastor, Bill Wilson, an amazing man with an amazing life story. He has written numerous books and produced numerous videos. Anyone thinking they have problems and want any encouragement to overcome them should read Bill's book *Whose Child is This?*—a truly gripping true story of a man's commitment to God's work. He has visited various cities in Britain, holding seminars about his Metro Ministries children's programme and advises how to get the programme initially started. Jacqui and I have attended two of his seminars in Liverpool and also went to Hackney, London, to help establish a mobile "Sidewalk Sunday School".

After the Metro Ministries experience in Bushwick, we returned to Clearwater, Florida on the 2nd of October 1995 and continued the involvement in our Calvary Baptist Church activities until we returned home on the 30th of November to celebrate Christmas at home for a change.

We helped with the children's Zone 3 project for 7 to 11 year olds run by the Boulevard Baptist Church members in partnership with Youth for Christ from May 1995 until April 2006, when Jacqui and I felt we had come to the end of our time at Zone 3. We were getting less mobile and older. During that time, nearly every year, at the school summer break, Jacqui and I sponsored a trip to Flamingo Animal and Amusement Park in North Yorkshire for the Zone 3 children who would be leaving us to go on to Secondary schools the following September. Some of the children became Christians, accepting Jesus as their Lord and Saviour. In recent years, in their late teens, Lee, Stacey and James, former Zone 3 participants, became so committed that they went on a mission to minister to street children in Bolivia, securing the funding by their own efforts and voluntary contributions, under the auspices of Youth With A Mission In Bolivia.

Our winter visits to Florida ended in 1997 because we had become more involved with the church programmes at home, and also due to Jacqui's degenerating medical condition. We keep in touch with our friends in Florida, exchanging cards and occasional phone calls.

Before I became a Christian, incidents happened in my life, which, at the time, I thought, "That was a lucky miss!" Since I became a Christian I realise that it could only have been God's intervention, known as Divine Intervention, or as some people say, "Their Guardian Angel." When I was on leave, Jacqui and I used to have a Saturday night out at a restaurant called The Four Winds near Driffield, run by Mr and Mrs Brown. On one occasion on our way home about midnight, we came to a crossroad. We had the right of way and the other road had stop signs. Just as we approached the junction a car crossed ahead of us. I had to violently wind the steering wheel to the right to avoid a potential horrific accident, which sent us careering towards a large tree. Two metres from the tree the car's engine stalled and we came to a full stop about one foot from disaster. I am convinced that was Divine Intervention. Also, in the incident when I was an Apprentice, we were in a hurricane and hadn't had sights to verify our position for several days, when the sun broke through the clouds for just a few minutes so we could establish a position line, which possibly averted a disaster. I now believe that was Divine Intervention. In Chapter Five, the incident of rescuing the people from the sinking yacht, I believe, was another manifestation of Divine Intervention: I'm sure those people would have been praying, even if it was only, "Oh God, what can we do now!"

Now that I am a Christian, I also believe that prayer is answered. On one occasion when I was docking the *Veracruz* in Antigua, I had miscalculated the strength of the wind and current and was heading straight towards another cruise ship, which was already docked. I was panicking and I said, "Oh God, what can I do now?" I don't know if I said it to myself or out loud, but a strange feeling of calm overcame me. I manoeuvred the engines, bow thrust propeller and helm as if it were someone else performing the operations. The passengers on the other ship were scattering and the crew were putting fenders out, then scattering as well. The *Veracruz* pulled up about a metre from the other ship and a catastrophe was avoided.

I also believe God speaks to us in different ways, as He did in my dream about not buying a new car and if you don't take notice, it happens anyway, because it's God's will.

Jacqui and I spend some time, first thing in the morning, reading daily devotional books, including *Day by Day with Billy Graham*. I had neglected for a couple of weeks to do any work on this autobiography, and then I read the Billy Graham reading for June the 15th, which was about Ephesians chapter 5 verse 16—"Redeeming the time." The prayer for the day at the end of the reading was: "Take away my procrastinating nature… how easy it is for me to waste time. I want to be able to leave a legacy of time spent for You, Lord, because that is eternal." I felt that was a gee-up for me to get started writing again!

In 1994, when we became members of the Boulevard Baptist Church, there were about 50 in the congregation at the Sunday services. Now in 2010 there are only about 15. Some people have moved on, out of the area. Some members holding office and others involved with the children's programmes have died unexpectedly in the prime of life, leaving a gaping hole in our membership. 95% of the membership of the church do not live in the Boulevard area of Hull but I believe they were directed there as Jacqui and I were. It seems inevitable, that if there are no new members coming into the church from the Boulevard area, the church will have to close, as several churches around the city of Kingston upon Hull have had to do. The church provides a service for the community, in that the Youth for Christ team use the premises and facilities to have a schoolchildren's breakfast club during term time and mums' special pampering night at the end of term time. Various groups such as mums and toddlers, neighbourhood watch, girls brigade, Zone 3 and Friday club for 5 to 7 year olds use the church buildings and facilities.

We need prayers that there will be a revival of Christian faith in the Boulevard area and that our church will be a beacon of light to lead believers into our church to the Glory of God.

Amen.

Appendix

i.   Savings Certificate..180

ii. Certificate of Merit for singing...180

iii. Tae-Kwon-Do Certificate Black Belt 1st Dan....................................181

iv. Trinity House School entrance record—just scraped in!...................182

v.   Letter from rescued people. 183

vi. Marriage Vows. 184

vii. Renewal of Marriage Vows..185

viii. Note to passengers. 186

ix. Bob Hope Menu...187

x.   HMS Bounty...188

xi. Dry Dock News 189

xii. Drew's Crews News 190

xiii. Map..191

1943 Savings Certificate

Certificate of Merit for singing

Tae-Kwon-Do Certificate Black Belt 1st Dan

REPORT AT ENTRANCE EXAMINATION....*5 March* 19 46

Applicants Register No. *1248*   Record Book No. *3131*

School Previously Attended   *Newington High School*

Report   *Birth 26 Nov 1932.*

Character: *Excellent*   Attendance: *313 of 341*

Punctuality: *lates.- nil*   Remarks: ————

Eyesight Examination Certificate Date   *22 Feb*   19 46

Personal Description :   Height: *5* Ft. *7½* Ins.

Colour of Eyes: *Brown*   Hair: *Dark Brown*

Complexion: *Dark*   Marks: ————

Entrance Examination Marks :

Dictation: *50*   Reading: *35*

Writing: *40*   Arithmetic: *65*

General Knowledge: *48* Personality: *100*

Merit Position: *34th.*

Probationary Period Commenced *18th. March*   19 46

   ,,   ,,   Completed   *8th. July*   19 46.

Each Report must be signed by the Parent and the Book returned
at the commencement of the succeeding term.

Trinity House School entrance record—just scraped in!

Letter from Janet & Jerry, one year after rescue.

MARRIAGE VOWS

S.S. "LIBERTE'"
IN FRENCH POLYNESIAN WATERS

_____ AND _____ HAVE INVITED YOU TO SHARE THE JOY OF THIS OCCASION AS THEY SEAL THE LOVE THEY SHARE IN THE EXCHANGE OF MARRIAGE VOWS. BE IT KNOWN TO ALL PRESENT THAT THIS IS NOT A LEGAL MARRIAGE._____ AND _____ INTEND LEGALIZING THIS MARRIAGE AT A LATER DATE.

_____ DO YOU TAKE _____ TO BE YOUR WIFE? DO YOU PROMISE TO LOVE HER AND CHERISH HER AS LONG AS YOU BOTH SHALL LIVE, IN THE BONDS OF HOLY MATRIMONY?

_____ DO YOU TAKE _____ TO BE YOUR HUSBAND? DO YOU PROMISE TO LOVE AND CHERISH HIM AS LONG AS YOU BOTH SHALL LIVE, IN THE BONDS OF HOLY MATRIMONY?

THE QUALITY OF LOVE IS BEAUTIFULLY EXPRESSED IN I CORINTHIANS 13. "IF I SPEAK IN THE TOUNGES OF MEN AND ANGELS, BUT DO NOT HAVE LOVE, I HAVE BECOME A NOISY GONG OR A CLANGING CYMBAL, AND IF I HAVE THE GIFT OF PROPHECY, AND KNOW ALL MYSTERIES AND ALL KNOWLEDGE: AND IF I HAVE FAITH, SO AS TO REMOVE MOUNTAINS, BUT DO NOT HAVE LOVE, I AM NOTHING. AND IF I GIVE ALL MY POSSESSIONS TO FEED THE POOR, AND IF I DELIVER MY BODY TO BE BURNED, BUT DO NOT HAVE LOVE, IT PROFITS ME NOTHING. LOVE IS PATIENT, LOVE IS KIND AND IS NOT ARROGANT, DOES NOT ACT UNBECOMINGLY, IT DOES NOT SEEK ITS OWN, IS NOT PROVOKED, DOES NOT TAKE INTO ACCOUNT A WRONGED SUFFERED, DOES NOT REJOICE IN UNRIGHTEOUSNESS, BUT REJOICES WITH TRUTH: BEARS ALL THINGS, HOPES ALL THINGS, ENDURES ALL THINGS, LOVE NEVER FAILS..."MAKE LOVE YOUR AIM"..

WILL YOU NOW JOIN YOUR RIGHT HANDS AND EXPRESS YOUR VOWS? I_____ TAKE YOU _____ TO BE MY WIFE. I DO PROMISE AND COVENANT, BEFORE GOD AND THESE WITNESSES, TO BE YOUR LOVING AND FAITHFUL HUSBAND, IN SICKNESS AND IN HEALTH, IN SORROW AS WELL AS IN JOY: IN WANT AS WELL AS IN PLENTY AND HEREIN I PLEDGE MY TRUTH.

I_____ TAKE YOU _____ TO BE MY HUSBAND, I DO PROMISE TO BE YOUR LOVING AND FAITHFUL WIFE, IN SICKNESS AS WELL AS HEALTH, IN SORROW AS WELL AS JOY, IN WANT AS WELL AS PLENTY AND HEREIN I PLEDGE MY TRUTH.

WHAT SYMBOL WILL YOU USE TO BIND YOUR PLEDGE? (A RING)

THIS RING IS MADE OF PRECIOUS METAL. LET IF SYMBOLIZE THE LOVE YOU SHARE AS THE MOST PRECIOUS PART OF YOUR MARRIAGE. AS A RING FORMS A CIRCLE WITH NO END, LET IT SYMBOLIZE A NEVER ENDING HONOR, RESPECT, FAITH AND TRUST TO CHARACTERIZE YOUR ENTIRE LIFE TOGETHER.

BLESS O LORD THIS RING AS _____ GIVES IT AND _____ WEARS IT. LET ITS SYMBOLISM BE A CONSTANT REALITY THROUGHOUT THEIR WEDDED LIFE.

THIS RING I GIVE YOU IN TOKEN AND PLEDGE OF MY CONSTANT FAITH AND ABIDING LOVE.

LET US PRAY: ALMIGHTY GOD, FATHER OF US ALL, YOUR LOVE HAS BROUGHT US INTO BEING AND BLESSES US IN ALL OF LIFE. LET YOUR LOVE BE THE EVERPRESENT UNITING POWER FOR _____ AND _____ THROUGHOUT THEIR LIFE TOGETHER. HENCEFORTH, LET THEIR THOUGHTS AND PLANS, THEIR JOYS AND SORROWS BE AS ONE. LET THEIR LOVE BE A BLESSING TO ALL WHO SHARE LIFE WITH THEM AND. IN YOUR HOLY NAME WE OFFER THIS PRAYER. AMEN.

MAY I HAVE YOUR RIGHT HANDS.

ALTHOUGH NOT A LEGAL MARRIAGE, I DECLARE THAT IN GOD'S SIGHT YOU ARE NOW HUSBAND AND WIFE. WHOM GOD HAS JOINED TOGETHER WITH HIS LOVE LET NO MAN PUT ASUNDER.

AS CAPTAIN OF THE S.S."LIBERTE'" I PLACE MY SEAL AND WITNESS TO THE EXCHANGE OF MARRIAGE VOWS MADE BY:

_____ AND _____

DATE: _____   MASTER: _____

CAPTAIN C. J. ANDERSON

Copy of Marriage Certificate issued to happy couple.

RENEWAL OF MARRIAGE VOWS

YOU THIS DAY _____ AND _____ HAVE INVITED TO SHARE THE JOY OF THIS OCCASION, AS THEY SEAL THE LOVE THEY SHARE, IN THE RENEWAL OF THEIR MARRIAGE VOWS, ORIGINALLY TAKEN

_____ TO BE YOUR WIFE? DO YOU PROMISE TO LOVE HER AS LONG AS YOU BOTH SHALL LIVE IN THE BONDS OF HOLY MATRIMONY? (ANSWER - I DO)

DO YOU TAKE _____ TO BE YOUR HUSBAND? DO YOU PROMISE TO LOVE AND CHERISH HIM AS LONG AS YOU BOTH SHALL LIVE, IN THE BONDS OF HOLY MATRIMONY? (ANSWER - I DO)

THE QUALITY OF LOVE IS BEAUTIFULLY EXPRESSED IN ONE CORINTHIANS, CHAPTER 13 - IF I SPEAK IN THE TONGUES OF MEN AND ANGELS, BUT DO NOT HAVE LOVE, I HAVE BECOME A GONG OR A CLANGING CYMBAL. AND IF I HAVE THE GIFT OF PROPHECY AND KNOW ALL MYSTERIES AND ALL KNOWLEDGE AND IF I HAVE FAITH, SO AS TO REMOVE MOUNTAINS, BUT DO NOT HAVE LOVE, I AM NOTHING. AND IF I GIVE ALL MY POSSESSIONS TO FEED THE POOR, AND IF I DELIVER MY BODY TO BE BURNED, BUT DO NOT HAVE LOVE, IT PROFITS ME NOTHING. LOVE IS PATIENT, LOVE IS KIND AND IS NOT ARROGANT, DOES NOT ACT UNBECOMINGLY, IT DOES NOT SEEK ITS OWN, IS NOT PROVOKED, DOES NOT TAKE INTO ACCOUNT A WRONG SUFFERED, DOES NOT REJOICE IN UNRIGHTEOUSNESS, BUT REJOICES WITH TRUTH, BEARS ALL THINGS, HOPES ALL THINGS, ENDURES ALL THINGS, LOVE NEVER FAILS.

WILL YOU NOW JOIN RIGHT HANDS AND EXPRESS YOUR VOWS REPEATING AFTER ME. I _____ TAKE YOU, _____ TO BE MY WIFE. I DO COVENANT BEFORE GOD AND THESE WITNESSES, TO BE YOUR LOVING AND FAITHFUL HUSBAND, IN SICKNESS AND IN HEALTH, IN SORROW AS WELL AS JOY, IN WANT AS WELL AS IN PLENTY AND HEREIN I PLEDGE MY TRUTH.

I _____ TAKE YOU, _____ TO BE MY HUSBAND I DO PROMISE TO BE YOUR LOVING AND

FAITHFUL WIFE, IN SICKNESS AS WELL AS IN HEALTH, IN SORROW AS WELL AS JOY, IN WANT AS WELL AS IN PLENTY AND HEREIN I PLEDGE MY TRUTH.

WHAT SYMBOL WILL YOU USE TO BIND YOUR PLEDGE? (ANSWER - A RING)

THIS RING IS MADE OF PRECIOUS METAL, LET IT SYMBOLIZE THE LOVE YOU SHARE AS THE MOST PRECIOUS PART OF YOUR MARRIAGE. AS A RING FORMS A CIRCLE WITH NO END, LET IT SYMBOLIZE A NEVER ENDING HONOR, RESPECT, FAITH AND TRUST TO CHARACTERIZE YOUR ENTIRE LIFE, TOGETHER.

BLESS O LORD THIS RING AS _____ GIVES IT AND _____ WEARS IT, LET ITS SYMBOLISM BE A CONSTANT REALITY THROUGHOUT THEIR WEDDED LIFE.

REPEAT AFTER ME, THIS RING I GIVE YOU IN TOKEN AND PLEDGE OF MY CONSTANT FAITH AND ABIDING LOVE.

LET US PRAY, ALMIGHTY GOD, FATHER OF US ALL, YOUR LOVE HAS BROUGHT US INTO BEING AND BLESSES US IN ALL OF LIFE. LET YOUR LOVE BE THE EVERPRESENT UNITING POWER FOR _____ AND _____ THROUGHOUT THEIR LIFE TOGETHER. HENCEFORTH, LET THEIR THOUGHTS AND PLANS, THEIR JOYS AND SORROWS BE AS ONE. LET THEIR LOVE BE A BLESSING TO ALL WHO SHARE LIFE WITH THEM AND IN YOUR HOLY NAME WE OFFER THIS PRAYER, AMEN.

CONGRATULATIONS TO YOU BOTH _____ YOU MAY KISS YOUR BRIDE.

Copy of Renewal of Marriage Vows Certificate.

BOB HOPE SHOW
FRIDAY, NOVEMBER 7, 1986
POOLSIDE, PROMENADE DECK, AFT

This week is a very special week for passengers aboard the S.S. LIBERTE. We are very lucky to have **Mr. Bob Hope** come aboard to tape part of his NBC Winter Tahiti Special, which will be televised in February, 1987. While he will be taping various skits throughout the islands, Mr. Hope will perform his famous monologue before S.S. LIBERTE passengers. Truly a special treat for us all!

In order to accomodate this special performance, we ask for your cooperation and understanding. Seating for S.S. Liberte passengers will begin at approximately 4:30 p.m. Due to space limitations, seating will be limited. However, there will also be standing room from other vantage points - along the Promenade Deck and Sun Deck railings. In the unlikely event of inclement weather, the show will be held in the Polynesian Room.

We hope you will enjoy this special onboard performance and that it will be one to add to your wonderful memories of French Polynesia. Your Farewell Dinner in the Tiare Dining Room on Friday will promise to be a memorable and enjoyable experience to complete your special week aboard S.S. Liberte. So as not to inconvenience you, the Bob Hope group will be accommodated in the Reef Restaurant, which will be closed from 3:30 p.m. to 8:30 p.m. Additionally, Le Club will be closed from 3:00 p.m. to 6:30 p.m. However, all other lounges and bars normally open during these hours, will be open to serve you.

We hope you are enjoying your week with us as well as the beautiful islands of French Polynesia.

Merci and maururu,

Captain Charles Anderson
Master, *S.S. Liberte*

Note to passengers.

Menu autographed by Bob Hope, Delores his wife, Jonathan Winters, Howard Keel, John Denver and Miss America 1986 Susan Akin.

H.M.S. BOUNTY

In 1787, the H.M.S. Bounty set sail from England, bound for Tahiti. The ship's mission was to transport breadfruit plants from Tahiti and her Islands to the West Indies. It was an arduous trip, made more difficult because of the strictness of its captain, William Bligh.

In this reproduction of Herb Kawainui Kane's painting of the famous Royal Navy vessel, much detail of the ship can be seen. It was small—only 91 feet long and 24 feet in beam. It boasted a copper bottom and a four pound cannon.

The riveting tale *Mutiny on the Bounty,* written by Charles Nordhoff and James Norman Hall, both military men, revolves around two powerful personalities, William Bligh and Fletcher Christian. When the Bounty encountered bitter storms at sea, it had no engines, no electronic instruments and no rescue helicopters, all of which we take for granted today.

The sailors endured food shortages and exhausting weeks of toil. Rather than encouraging his crew, Bligh was angry, paranoid and raged mercilessly at them.

When the Bounty finally arrived in Tahiti, the crew found the island to be a great comfort. The food was delicious and the women were hospitable. The crew remained on the island for several months, recuperating before setting sail for home.

On the return trip, Bligh became more overbearing, and more unreasonable than ever. His men, still filled with memories of their time in Tahiti, found his behavior less and less tolerable. They reached the breaking point and rose in mutiny.

The rest of this true story is history and was chronicled in several motion pictures.

American Hawaii Cruises

One of the outer covers of the daily menus.

Rescue tug works near cruise ship in shipyard.   UPI PHOTO

Rude awakening in dry dock:
31 injured as ship rolls over

The Washington Post

NORFOLK, Va. — Rey Bautista, a 29-year-old second mate on a Caribbean cruise ship, woke up early Monday on the deck of his cabin. Confused, he climbed back into his bunk, only to discover he couldn't lie down without holding on.

"I thought I was dreaming," he said. Then he heard cries of "What happened?" echoing from the passageways and watched as a light in his cabin flickered out.

What happened was that his ship, the 491-foot Vera Cruz I, had lurched sideways on its steel and wooden platform in a dry dock here, spilling the crew of 142 from their bunks and injuring 31, one critically.

The vessel, which had been placed in the dry dock 7½ hours earlier for a routine hull check, slid 35 degrees to starboard at 3:40 a.m., with a crash that one witness likened to a sonic boom.

SHIPYARD spokesmen could give no immediate explanation for the accident, which snapped lines securing the ship, buckled a metal gangplank and crushed a 30-foot wooden wall next to the ship. The wall and a pier broke the ship's slide. Rescue workers said it was miracle that more people were not seriously injured.

Crew members of the Panamanian-registered ship, many in their underwear and night clothes, fought their way up darkened, steeply angled passageways to the ship's top decks, then jumped or slid down lines to safety on the pier.

"It just happened so quick," said Sylvia Ventimeglia, 38, the first purser on the 27-year-old ship. "I was awakened by a creaking sound and I said 'Whoa,' to myself, 'something is happening here.' Seconds after the creaking, it was over. It was the sound of like wood breaking."

Early indications pointed to a problem with the aged, wooden and steel platform on which the ship was perched. Coast Guard Lt. Cmdr. Chris Walter of the Hampton Roads Marine Safety Office said he found no evidence of any shift in the Vera Cruz's weight that could have caused the accident.

Once the ship heeled over, it breached a wall of the dry dock, which became flooded. By dawn the Vera Cruz had righted itself to 11 degrees.

NASH BILISOLY, an attorney for Norfolk Shipbuilding and Drydock Corp., the private yard where the accident occurred, said the shipyard is waiting for an official report from the Coast Guard before commenting.

William Birkhead, another shipyard attorney, said a watchman checked the dry dock 10 minutes before the accident and found everything in order.

Shipyard officials said it was the first time a ship had ever fallen in a dry dock in the 69 years that the yard has been operating along the Southern Branch of the Elizabeth River opposite downtown Portsmouth.

The Vera Cruz I, owned by the Bahama Cruise Line Inc. of New York, regularly sails between Florida and Mexico during the winter. The ship, which carries a crew and passengers numbering more than 1,000, had entered the yard here Sunday afternoon after a cruise from Montreal to New York.

The accident toppled chairs, threw ashtrays through the air and rolled a piano across a room.

Thirty-one crew members were taken to three area hospitals. All but one were treated and released. Avery Darling, a Jamaican room steward, was admitted to Norfolk General Hospital with head injuries, a hospital spokeswoman said. Darling, who remains unconscious, is in critical condition, she said.

Newspaper report of the capsizing in dry dock.

Volume I
Edition 12
April 18, 1986

****

LETTER FROM THE EDITOR

I would like to dedicate this issue of the paper to the late Drew Farion. (By late I mean overdue). It seems tht again I find myself in the Editor's seat, and that, of course, means I get to say whatever I want!!! Well, the only thing I want to say is: Captain Anderson, you're the best. Have a wonderful vacation and come back to us soon. I have had the pleasure of sailing with several Captains in my career with AHC, and never before have I enjoyed working underanyone as much as I have with Captain Anderson. Charlie is about as nice a guy as I ever hope to meet. He epitomizes the phrase "An officer and a gentleman!" He has never been too busy to listen, nor to preoccupied to care. He has instilled a comoradrie amongst the officers and crew the like of which has never been seen on either of the other two ships. If credit is due to any one factor for the incredible ratings this ship has received in the short time we have been sailing, then it goes to Captain Anderson as Master of the S.S. Liberte (he would take the credit anyway!) We the officers, staff and crew of the NUMBER ONE ship in American Hawaii Cruises salute you. God bless and send you back to us soon,

Sincerely,
R.H.

P.S. Captain Bourke, we want you to know that you're not exactly chopped liver yourself!!!

P.S.S. Special thanks to Sandi and Jackie for contributing their typing efforts this week as guest publishers.

FROM THE CAPTAIN'S SEA CHEST
THE STATE OF THE NATION, ESPECIALLY THE LIBERTE'

We did it! 3.84 and broke the record for the highest guest comment card score in the history of American Hawaii Cruise Line vessels. Congratulations to all. It was nice for it to happen when Mr. and Mrs. Jesse were on the Liberte' to witness it and they were as pleased as I. Captain Ricconi, Captain Yip and all the Papeete office were thrilled as well. The impromptu champagne celebration in the Polynesian Showroom was well attended. There will be a party on Saturday from 12 noon to 2pm, by the pool area. No throwing in the pool please. For those personnel who cannot attend the party on Saturday, there will be a motu party next Wednesday in Raiatea. The party advertised for this Wednesday had to be cancelled due to all the sporting activities. The company has an incentive program for the vessels who attain a guest comment card score over 3.59, as follows:

A score over 3.59 paid $0.50 per guest
"   "   "   3.75 " $1.00 "   "
"   "   "   3.90 " $2.00 "   "

The cash goes to the crew recreation fund. From the 3 times we have passed the target we have $1308.50 into the fund. It looks as though we can get a regular donation from the way things have come together. It's not impossible to obtain that $2.00 per guest incentive. I wonder what it is for 4.0?

As usual an invitation is extended to those personnel going on vacation this Saturday, to attend the informal cocktail party in my cabin at 4:30pm Friday. I am going on vacation this Saturday until June 14th. Captain Bourke is taking over for the 2 months and I'm sure you will give him the co-operatin you have given me and will keep those guest comment card scores way up there.

On behalf of the whole crew I wish to thank Mr. Jesse and Captain Ricconi for the congratulatory telex messages.

Crew member of the week was Felimon Redidor, 2nd Cook who has always been hard working and I have never seen him without a smile on his face, a ray of sunshine, which is needed sometimes in the hot galley.

(continued on page 2)

First page of Edition 12 of Drew's *Crews News.*

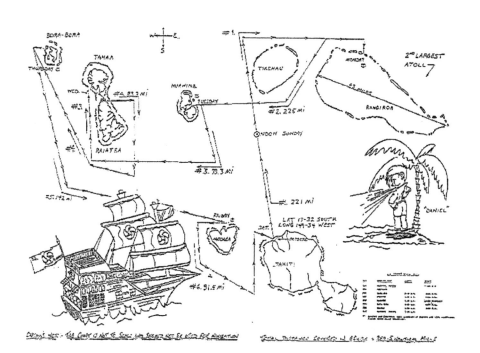

Map

Lightning Source UK Ltd.
Milton Keynes UK
22 November 2010

163249UK00002B/271/P